Dear God, Have You Ever Gone Hungry?

Dear God, Have You Ever Gone Hungry?

Memoirs by

Joseph Bau

Translated from the Hebrew by Shlomo "Sam" Yurman

 Arcade Publishing • New York

FIRST ENGLISH-LANGUAGE EDITION 1998

Library of Congress Cataloging-in-Publication Data

Ba'u, Yosef.
    [Shenot 698. English]
    Dear God, have you ever gone hungry? : memoirs / by Joseph Bau ;
translated from the Hebrew by Shlomo "Sam" Yurman. —1st English-
language ed.
      p.   cm.
    ISBN 1-55970-431-4
    1. Ba'u, Yosef. 2. Jews—Persecutions—Poland—Krakow. 3. Holocaust,
Jewish (1939–1945)—Poland—Krakow—Personal narratives. 4. Krakow
(Poland)—Ethnic relations. I. Title.
DS135.P62K6789313 1998
940.53'18'094386—dc21   98–17133

*Frontispiece: portrait of Joseph and Rebecca Bau, with their camp uniforms sketched in
by Joseph Bau*

All the artwork reproduced in this book is by Joseph Bau.

Published in the United States by Arcade Publishing, Inc., New York
Distributed by Little, Brown and Company

10 9 8 7 6 5 4 3 2 1

Designed by API

BP

PRINTED IN THE UNITED STATES OF AMERICA

I dedicate this book to my beloved wife Rebecca, and thank her for our beautiful 53 years together. —SBart

To the memory of my beloved wife, Rebecca, who died on April 28, 1997. We lived together for fifty-three years, through thick and thin. Only thanks to her was I able to write and illustrate this and other books. When we celebrated our fiftieth wedding anniversary, many in the press and on television represented us as the most romantic couple on earth. We had married in great secrecy in the Plaszow concentration camp, and by now almost the whole world knew of it and honored us for it. By coincidence, though we weren't aware of this in the camp, the wedding took place on Valentine's Day, the international day of love.

This book is also dedicated to the memory of

My mother, Tzilah Bau,
murdered in Bergen-Belsen in 1945

My father, Abraham Bau,
murdered in the Plaszow concentration camp in 1943

My brother Iziu (Ignacy) Bau,
murdered in the Krakow ghetto in 1943

The six million Jews
who perished with them

Oskar Schindler,
without whom this book would never have been written,
who died in Frankfurt in 1974

Contents

I am not responsible for the contents.
I copied them straight from life.

Dear God,
Have You Ever
Gone Hungry?

In the middle of the summer of 1939, I went with my mother to the market to shop for fruit. After carefully examining almost every stand, Mother stopped at one presided over by a rather corpulent woman and asked, "How much for these apples?"

Despite her sumptuous build, the woman quoted a lean price: "Twenty groschen a kilo."

Since it was customary for the vendors there to inflate their prices in order to leave room for bargaining, Mother assumed she was expected to follow the ritual. "Won't you take fifteen groschen for these rejects?" she asked.

The fat woman rose from her stack of sacks, lifted her pudgy hands toward the cloudy sky, and intoned a prayer: "O God, who art in heaven, pour down a hail of fire upon these terrible people."

Overcome by fear, we ran home with empty shopping bags. A few weeks later the war broke out, and bombs started raining down on Krakow from the sky. As Mother collapsed in terror, I asked with unconcealed irony, "Well, Mom, did it pay to bring about all this calamity for your five groschen?"

THE HOUSE THAT WAS

There was a house once,
and in this house each tenant lived in a private world,
where secrets and memories crowded within decorated walls . . .

Until the strangers came to destroy this world.
They tore off the roof and, without anesthetic,
began to yank the walls apart, brick by brick.

Doors stood agape in confusion,
windows were blinded in their sleep,
electricity died in a tangle of copper wires,
walls collapsed and ceilings plunged down,
corners vanished, and the streets were strewn
with priceless heirlooms and the souls of battered relics
and heaps of possessions laden with memories.

People rummaging in the rubble for past worlds
spread their arms in helpless sorrow:
"Where are our treasures now?"
Men wept and women, their young clinging to their skirts,
scratched away at the mounds with their fingernails
to recover some precious remnant.

Nearby houses looked on with indifference,
as one of their own was wiped from the map.
Neighbors scoured the texts of the sages
to find some reason or rhyme for one building's destruction,

hoping the sacrifice would serve their salvation.
And no man tried to intervene,
for fear of risking his immunity . . .

Until the strangers rolled up their sleeves outside his house.

A HANUKKAH MIRACLE

It happened in occupied Krakow some two years after the start of World War II. Having removed the Jewish population from the protection of the law, the Germans proceeded toward their Final Solution of total annihilation. A curfew was enforced between the hours of 9 P.M. and 6 A.M. Jews were banned from trains and streetcars and ordered to wear armbands with a blue Star of David on a white background. The children were expelled from the local schools, and every Jew had to carry a *Kennkarte,* a yellow identity card issued by the police.

Yet some Jews were denied these cards, which made them subject to immediate deportation by way of the infamous "transports." My brother Marcel and I belonged to this group. With the aid of pull and a large sum of money, our father managed to procure forged cards for us from the regional council in Olsha, a village on the outskirts of the city. These would pass casual inspection, but if they were discovered to be fakes, we would incur the usual punishment — a bullet in the head.

After a frantic search for lodging in the village, we arranged for the use of a couch in the home of a Christian chimney sweep, at an exorbitant monthly rent. However, this was available only between 9 P.M. and 8 A.M. In the daytime, we were forced to roam Olsha's lanes and byways.

The locals regarded us with a mixture of fear and outright hostility. Their fear was due to the danger to their lives should they be found aiding or cooperating with Jews. On the other hand, the proximity of a military air base caused them to mistrust strangers of any sort. No one bothered to ask for our identity or place of abode, but we were aware of people's scrutiny at our every step.

It was an unusual winter. At times, a frosty wind covered the ground with sleet; on other days, our wretched world was engulfed by a cold Siberian gale that spread mounds of snow and thick layers of solid ice. We envied the fortunate ones who were safely in their homes.

With no place to seek shelter until the night, Marcel and I were forced to stay outdoors. Soaked to the bone and shivering from cold, we trudged through the snow and limped over the sparkling ice, until we felt our brains solidify from the frost. To keep our spirits up, we chatted about the pleasures of life before the war. We tried exchanging jokes and even managed to laugh a little. However, the bitter reality soon overcame our attempts at levity and turned them into macabre jests, too gruesome for words.

Each afternoon, we lingered behind a kiosk, opposite the last streetcar stop, to await the arrival of our younger brother, ten-year-old Iziu, who would bring us a pot of soup and a summary of the latest news. He didn't look particularly Jewish, so he didn't stand out among his fellow travelers. However, a sudden check of identity papers or a denunciation by some suspicious passenger could easily have cost him his life.

After we had endured the freezing outdoors for three months, Iziu came with the usual pot of soup and some disturbing news — all the Jews were being ordered to move into the ghetto. Our parents asked us to come home in order to help pack what was left of our possessions.

That night, in violation of the racial laws and the curfew, we removed the Star of David armbands and boarded a streetcar. Marcel sat in the front row behind the driver, while I chose the last row, near the exit. That way, at least one of us would be able to jump out in the event of a Nazi trap. Ordinarily, the ride into the city took no more than half an hour, but on that particular night, time seemed to be standing still, and the streetcar, as if in cahoots with our persecutors, traveled at a snail's pace. I tried staring out the window, but all I could see were the reflections of the other passengers and the car's interior. Behind my calm facade, my heart was in my throat, and only the sound of the wheels on the tracks was louder than the throbbing of the blood in my veins.

Oh, how we longed to see Mother, Father, Iziu, and our apartment! At home, they welcomed us back like brave heroes — not with medals but with an avalanche of kisses. For the first time in three months, we enjoyed the luxury of a home-cooked meal and the ecstasy of a warm bath.

After two years of German plunder and confiscations, there was precious little to pack. Nevertheless, it took a whole night and day to prepare our memory-laden household for the move. Father was spared much of the unhappy chore, since he went out before dawn to look for transport. If only he could find a way to move the beloved coziness of our youth to the ghetto!

This was turning out to be a lucrative season for those who

owned some means of transport. They turned the Jews' misfortune to profit, and no price was too high, no conditions were unreasonable.

That evening we carried our dearest belongings downstairs and loaded them into a farm wagon that was attached to a miserable, bony nag and normally used to haul manure to the fields. We bade a hasty good-bye to the apartment, and without the appropriate eulogies, Father surrendered the key to the caretaker. Such was our parting! A few more words, a few tears, another look at the third-floor windows, and a few final kisses, perhaps really final — who could know? A long, gloomy night lay ahead of us, without the prospect of any improvement in the morning. . . .

Mother, Father, and Iziu trailed behind the squealing, smelly wagon, as if forming a funeral procession for our relics on their last journey, to the Krakow ghetto. Marcel and I discreetly removed the armbands from our sleeves again and boarded a streetcar. Our return trip was uneventful. Afraid of being caught by the approaching curfew, we replaced the armbands as soon as we got off and hurried toward some relief on the rented couch, at least until the morning.

Just then, a Jew, thoroughly soaked, darted out of the darkness and, without stopping, warned us that an SS man was posted on the bridge ahead and was plunging any Jew who wanted to cross into the deep waters of the river. Without asking for details, we hastily reversed direction and began to run. All at once, it dawned on us that we had no place to go. The apartment was no longer ours; it was locked and the key in the hands of the caretaker, who had never been fond of Jews. Our family was by now in the ghetto, which it was impossible to enter at this late hour, especially without proper documents. We found ourselves on a strange street, with the curfew breathing down our necks.

Instead of achieving the hoped-for security of our rented couch, we were obliged to remove the armbands again and risk the consequences. We desperately needed an alternate route to our vil-

lage. In order to avoid suspicion, we proceeded at a leisurely pace. On entering the first side street, though, we became engulfed by total darkness and quickly lost our sense of direction.

One thing was certain: We couldn't risk the danger of asking anyone for help. We had to find another bridge, if one existed, and keep away from the air base.

In order to be taken for local residents, we decided to act like a couple of drunks, reeling unsteadily and shouting curses and obscenities at each other. Marcel walked ahead; I trailed behind. The black darkness, our utter confusion, and the fear of encountering anti-Semites helped us to express ourselves in a most foul and disgusting manner.

"Drop dead, you dirty sonofabitch, but first give me back the money you owe me," I yelled. "Screw you, you crazy bastard. Shut up before I bash your goddamn head in," Marcel countered. This is only a weak translation from the Polish, a language blessed with Russian expletives that are almost impossible to render into English.

All at once, without warning, we were confronted by a band of young thugs brandishing sticks and clubs. Their apparent leader turned the beam of a flashlight in my face, which was still contorted by the words I was mouthing, and, manifestly satisfied, shouted to his gang, "Look, boys, these can't be dirty Jews — they're just like us. Let them go!" It had worked! Relieved, we continued to stumble and curse, blessing our intimate knowledge of obscenities.

Wearily, we kept lifting our tired legs, not knowing where they would lead us. Only by the rustling of the reeds and the sloshing of the mud under our feet did we know we had left the main road and entered an open field. Nearby, we could hear the sounds of the river, whose banks were caressed by the flow. It seemed so near but beyond our reach in the starless night.

Ready to leap back to safety at any sign of danger, I pressed forward, gingerly placing one foot ahead of the other and testing the ground. Marcel trudged behind me, still cursing at the top of his lungs while trembling with fear: "Cruddy river, you sonofabitch, I hope you dry up and die of thirst! I hope the goddamn fish drink you up to the last drop!"

Soon we heard a hum of motors and the muffled voices of the workers in their shops. Through the fog, we perceived that we were close to the air base, which seemed to be full of activity. Suddenly, we saw in the distance a faint light trying to pierce the darkness.

Like a sailor in the crow's nest of his ship, I began shouting, "Land ho! Dry land ahead!" We were beyond caring what lay behind the flickering light. Our only thought was to end our impossible predicament, to emerge from the dark belly of the whale that seemed to have swallowed the entire world. With our last ounce of strength, we advanced toward the beckoning gleam.

"Look, I can see a pair of candles," I exclaimed. "If I'm not mistaken, this is the first night of Hanukkah. Maybe we've reached a Jewish home." With the echoes of a distant past sounding in my ears, I began humming the words of the prayer "Maoz Tsur Yeshuati," a melody long forgotten, which brought a spark of life to two young men on the edge of despair.

We reached a fence and slowly circled the house behind it. Then wonder of wonders! We were at the house of the chimney sweep whose couch we were renting. A tall man whose face bore a mustache opened the door and expressed surprise at our late arrival and mud-soaked condition.

Then he added, "There's been a power failure in the village tonight. Go to the kitchen and take one of the lit candles."

To this day, I'm unable to explain how we managed to reach that house in the gloomy night, how we crossed the river and the air base without being aware of it. After the war, I returned to the place several times, trying to discover the route that had led us toward the two burning candles, but my efforts were to no avail. The mystery can only be explained as our private Hanukkah miracle.

THE SECRET

Like an oil slick in a sea of milk,
the street melts leisurely.
Streetlamps, enveloped in a veil of mist,
relay to each other their yellowish gleam
and scatter lost rays on the sidewalks.
Houses open windows in confusion and draw aside.
Passersby glance with amazement.

I am walking
without touching the hostile zone.
I am walking,
but shh, to say where is forbidden,
because *he* is in every corridor,
clad in night's black uniform,
hiding in every corner,
in every doorway lurking like an ambush.

In an instant, my shadow might collapse on a wall, but
I am walking,
with my heart ensnared in the noose of my tie.
I am walking
without the Star of David on my sleeve.

If only I could erase from my face
the fear of a hunted animal,
or walk a straight line on my rubbery feet,
or not tempt the noses of the gendarmes
with the scent of some careless prey.

BLACKOUT SCREENS

W hile confined within the ghetto walls, we tried to maintain a semblance of normalcy, each within the routines of his occupation and according to his ingrained habits. However, in that atmosphere of murder and violence, it became necessary to seek new horizons. For example, professionals like lawyers, judges, and administrators were forbidden to practice their vocations. The new masters had no need for experts in law and justice; rabbis, teachers, university lecturers, and any others connected with cultural or educational activities were hounded and hunted down. Nobody dared to admit to even a slight involvement in those spheres. Midwives and circumcisers became obsolete; apparently, infants deemed it prudent to wait out this period of madness before emerging into the world. In any case, no pregnant women were seen in the ghetto.

The regime of terror offered instead demeaning and despicable careers, as Kapos — Jewish policemen who wielded whips and rained vile curses upon their own people — and paid informers and traitors in other forms, who helped the oppressors, hoping in vain to save their own skins.

Learned, respected men, deprived of dignity, clung to diplomas stored in mothballs among the family papers, hoping that someday they might become useful again. To remind them of their vanished glory, I would address the stationery merchant, saying, "Herr Professor, may I have a lined notepad?" or I would ask the dirty, perspiring fuel dealer, "A bucket of coal, please, Herr Advocat."

My mother, a certified couturier, owned a millinery boutique that employed five women in the center of the city. Thanks to her specialty, she was given a temporary permit to stay alive. Later, she was accorded the honor of sharing the misery of the other ghetto dwellers, but despite this she received a pass to leave the ghetto for the purpose of running her business outside. Before we were forced to change our address, her hat salon had been a single tram stop or a ten-minute walk away. But after the Germans sealed off the ghetto walls in order to protect the Aryan race from epidemics and other caprices of nature arising from the squalor within, the distance between us and the store was four kilometers, and my mother had to have herself driven there in a closed carriage. The reason? The wearers of Star of David armbands were not allowed to use the trams.

One black day in our family annals, a female custodian of seized properties appropriated the keys to the boutique as well as Mother's license, and a swastika replaced the Star of David in the window. Thus my mother lost her status as a "cruel international

capitalist who sucked the blood of her slaves," to become instead an unpaid, expendable worker in her own shop. Besides losing her meager salary, she was deprived of all benefits, which included the carriage rides. In order to maintain a dubious claim on her business and her contact with the outside world, she rose at dawn and walked the four kilometers to her place of nominal employment. This enabled her to obtain provisions to feed our insatiable appetites. At night, dead tired, she trudged the same four kilometers back to the ghetto, carrying her skimpy ration of food. On rainy days she got soaked to the bone, and in the winter the cold turned her into a block of ice. In her total humiliation, with tears sometimes staining her agonized face, Mother persisted stubbornly in retaining a glimmer of hope, which was sustained only by the memory of happy days in the not so distant past. But on another black day in our family annals, she was deprived of her pass and posted to hard labor in the warehouse of former Jewish belongings.

My father was just a father, without further adjectives. We loved and respected him unreservedly for what he was. Being in ill health, he obtained with his *Kennkarte* an exemption from the "transports." With ironical pride, he showed us the doctor's letter and commented, "Thank God I'm dying." My two brothers, Marcel and Iziu, became students in retirement. According to Hitler, they and other Jewish youths had been born only for forced labor, which didn't require an educated upbringing. At first, they welcomed this relief from early-morning rising, the hope of a holiday due to the teacher's illness, and parental scolding for poor marks. After a while, however, the luster of idleness faded away. Especially after the Germans conscripted them to sweep the streets, before assigning them to hard labor in construction. That's when they developed a sudden longing for school and learning, but it was to no avail.

Owing to our parents' foresight, which led them to seek to

equip each child with some skill or vocation, I had learned the trade of draftsman. Although lacking a diploma, I became proficient enough to earn some money, even if it was a pittance. As fate had it, this skill would later save me from certain death. However, my calling was not entered on any document, as both Marcel and I were not accorded "citizenship" in the ghetto. We had no *Kennkarten*. We had no *protekzia* (pull) or funds to bribe the officials who issued these passports to hell, which conferred on the bearer the lofty title of *Jude* and obliged him to wear an armband with a Star of David. Undocumented, we belonged to the lowliest, most despicable class in the countries controlled by the German empire.

According to the Nazis' holy bible, *Mein Kampf,* Jews were subhuman creatures, without any civil rights. Nevertheless, the Jewish presence had to be taken into account as an obvious administrative fact, except in the case of those, like us, who had no official existence. Since our names weren't listed anywhere, we were subject to immediate deportation to an unknown destination if we were caught during the daily and nightly "actions." At that time, the many stories about special genocide installations and incinerators were still treated as mere rumors.

In plain language, my brother and I had entered the ghetto illegally and lived there without permission from the SS or the local chief of police. We had no ration books issued by the Krakow municipality, no residence permits from the Jewish Community Council *(Judenrat).* This made us parasites, exploiting the tenuous rights of our parents and little Iziu. Under the prevailing conditions, we occupied a small, dingy room together, without electricity, running water, or a toilet. This room was located in a gloomy hut situated at No. 1 Plac Zgody — Peace Square, in Polish. What an irony!

A few days after Mother smuggled us into the ghetto, I ventured outside to assess our grim new reality. My first impression gave me a frightening insight. I noticed that the Germans had painstakingly copied from the Middle Ages not only the term "ghetto" but also the way the poor creatures destined to live there should be confined. Medieval woodcuts had obviously inspired the builders of the modern-day enclosures, and they had constructed a tall, fortified wall to hide from the eyes of the world the atrocities that were to be inflicted on the Jews and the crimes against their property.

A formidable stronghold, with walls built of bricks held together by hatred, the ghetto was designed to hold a population of Jews in unbelievably crowded conditions. Every room was occupied by several families, each of them with a few pieces of furniture and

an assortment of worries and problems. One kitchen served all these families, so its use had to be scheduled by the hour. A line of impatient people, some unable to contain themselves, always waited outside the toilet. In houses facing the outside walls, the ground-floor windows were blocked up, and no daylight could enter. The main gates were also closed off, so an unofficial visitor to the ghetto had to seek devious ways of gaining admission, through byways never planned by the city engineers.

At times, it was necessary to cross several filthy courtyards cluttered with discarded furniture and to pass through abandoned stairways and the corridors of adjoining houses. No one asked for permission to trespass, and no one objected. On a bright day, you could read the street names and numbers with difficulty; in the evening it became worse, and at night it was virtually impossible. The community council ignored the comfort of the inhabitants, failing to provide sanitation, legible street signs, and minimal illumination. Every "tenant" acted according to his needs and desires and justifiably paid no heed to the authorities.

I did my best to adapt to these cruel circumstances. I tried to find someone of influence among the residents I knew, but all my friends and acquaintances regarded me with indifference and let me know by their expressions that they were sorry, but my face was unfamiliar and my voice sounded odd. My former classmates suffered from some form of amnesia: they remembered something but only through the fog in their brain or from some previous incarnation. Yes, someone like me had been in their class, but that was a long time ago. . . . Yet scarcely two years had passed since we played daring pranks together!

Even my closest girlfriends dismissed the intimacies of our common youth, because romance had given way to more significant matters. The clerks at the community offices acted like purebred Germans and vented their anger at me before shutting the door in my face. I laid eyes for the first time on these renegades in their monster costumes — the neat uniforms of the Jewish police. They called themselves the Service of Order *(Ordnung Dienst)* — a curse on their order! I tried to adjust to this surrealistic world, but with no success.

Following a futile search for occasional work and a humiliating effort to get a *Kennkarte*, which would permit me to join the others abandoned by God, I decided to go independent and hung up a sign, APPLIED GRAPHIC ART, in the window of our room. Many people were puzzled by the meaning of these magic words, while the linguists among them failed to see a connection between the sign and its location. Did anyone caught in this maelstrom have a need for applied graphic art, of all things? And if so, what purpose would it serve in this one-way lane to the slaughterhouse? Even I didn't have an answer.

Well, I started drawing cards to post on apartment doors in order to discourage the German and Jewish police from entering, or at least to lessen the damage if they did enter. What magic could my signs perform? My idea was to draw, on white card stock the size of a postcard, the full name of the customer in black Gothic lettering positioned between two red rules. In the middle of a second line, in smaller print, went "Employed by:" followed below by the name of his workplace in bold print. All the Jews in the ghetto, except illegals like us, were in the employ of the Third Reich, which farmed them out through employment offices to public institutions like the army and the police or anyone else willing to pay for their services and so add to the coffers of the mighty German State. Generally, Jews were not put to work as managers or even minor clerks. They were assigned the hardest unskilled labor, and their employers were entitled to demand from the workers branded with the name *Jude* the maximum effort in the maximum period of time. They were even permitted to kick and literally tear apart anyone who failed or seemingly refused to do a job, and they didn't have to report it or give a rational reason.

The poor hapless slaves outdid themselves in performing impossible tasks under inhuman conditions. Their pay was a liter of watery soup and the illusion that their assistance to the Reich's war effort might reduce their death sentences to life imprisonment — i.e., to imprisonment until the end of the war. People even paid bribes to officials and *Machers* in order to obtain work at some influential company for the lifesaving benefit it might provide.

Subsequently, they would order a sign with their name bordered in red over the name of the hallowed employer, in the hope that the mention of the firm in the Gothic script that was holy to the Nazis would somehow protect them and their families. In the end, my invention proved worthless. During the "actions," the bullets failed to spare the owners of even the finest signs.

One day, I had an unusual customer. Instead of the official door sign, he ordered a large poster advertising blackout curtains. I asked for more details, so I could paint an illustration for the poster promoting this revolutionary invention. His idea was simple but utilitarian; it would replace the blankets and various cardboard sheets and papers that people used to cover their windows so British and Russian pilots wouldn't bomb the ghetto. The device was a curtain made of black paper that could be used and removed as needed.

"Here is how it works," he went on to explain, as he took out two pencils and a piece of black paper. "First you attach this paper to a round wooden rod with small nails and you roll it up like this; then you attach it to a flat stick to which you screw three little pulleys — here, here, and here. Then you thread a piece of rope through the pulleys, like this. The ends of the ropes are tied together outside." He straightened the black scroll and rolled it up again a few times. "You see, it's very simple but ingenious. Anyone can operate it, or even make it himself."

As I was working on the poster, Marcel looked on with the eyes of an expert, mumbling to himself. Then he proclaimed with a broad smile, "This is a fantastic idea. It's exactly what I've been looking for. Easy to manufacture, very little material required, and a chance to make a fortune. Please remove your inks and brushes from this table; we're going to start producing our own blackout curtains. Remember, our parents need our help. Just make one extra sign, and we'll post it in place of your Graphics sign. In a few days, people will be standing in line to order these curtains from us."

After a moment's reflection, he added, "Just change the name to something more appealing. Screen ... blind. ... No, I have it: blackout rollers — because soon the money will be rolling in and we'll be rich!"

I was so sure Marcel was kidding that I didn't bother to give him a lecture on honesty, ethics, and patent rights. Instead, I set to work with a vengeance, relishing the escape from our bitter reality. I designed beautiful lettering and sketched a window true to the model, but with an air of gaiety. Before pasting the sketch on the poster, I added a bottle with a blue flower to the sill. As I proudly viewed my work, I forgot about the war and our fight for survival. Time stood still momentarily, and people assumed a semblance of normalcy in these abnormal surroundings.

My work of art complete, I wrapped it with care and went to deliver it to my special customer. I didn't have far to go, as distances in the ghetto were quite small. In fact, everyone was a close neighbor. The inventor of the blackout curtain lived in a dank, crowded basement room with his family of several children, a few adults, and some old people. Their living conditions were even worse than ours.

He liked my poster, and without taking time to admire my artistry and the quality of the work, he rushed outside and hung it on the house. No one offered me any refreshment, as that kind of hospitality had long gone out of style in the ghetto. In plain fact, there was nothing to offer. The man also neglected to ask about my fee — he just promised to pay me when he sold the first curtain.

I walked the short distance home very slowly, trying to size up my situation. After all, things were looking up. I had my drafting table, my work was interesting, and we had a window that admitted both light and air. Things could have been a lot worse. In my reverie, our tiny room became a spacious, elegant apartment.

That illusion was rudely shattered as soon as I entered our home. I had to go out and look at the sign again to make sure that I hadn't entered the neighbor's room by mistake. My "studio" was beyond recognition. The tabletop, which had been set at an incline for drafting, was now level, and my work implements, the inks, paints, pens, brushes, and white card stock, had been replaced by a messy array of black paper, nails, screws, a broken hammer, and a pair of rusty pliers. My artistic aura had given way to a pungent smell of carpenter's glue and deafening noise. Marcel was sitting in my chair, trying to make a blackout screen that would be simpler, cheaper, and more efficient. Wielding a razor, he hacked away at the black paper with such fury that he sent chips flying from the surface of my precious drafting board. I vented my anger on the poor door of our room, slamming it with all my might.

Marcel ignored my anger. Without looking up from his work, he asked in a mocking voice, "Nu, how did they like your poster?" I answered meekly, "They liked it very much." He continued sarcastically on my behalf: "Oh, yes. As usual, 'I finished, delivered, and got no payment' — isn't it so?"

After a few days, my lovely sign was replaced by one crudely lettered by Marcel, but I had to admit that the text was more likely to attract attention. It proclaimed: ROLLER CURTAIN — THE NEW INVENTION ENDORSED BY EXPERTS. AN AUTOMATIC SCREEN AT A BARGAIN PRICE. EXCLUSIVE DISTRIBUTORS. True to Marcel's prediction, people began to line up in front of our house, anxious to place their orders. As an important assistant to the manufacturer, I toiled zealously to produce the rollers. Marcel handled the administrative side, accepting orders, purchasing materials, and, most important, collecting the money. Success went to his head, and he took himself to be an astute businessman and an able manager of his staff of one — yours truly.

Somehow we procured a permit to buy a roll of good-quality black paper, but when we got it, we decided it would be a pity to cut it up. So instead, Marcel sold it on the black market and obtained in

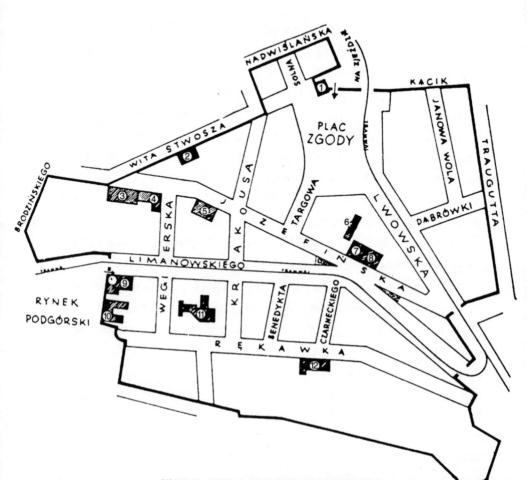

THE KRAKOW GHETTO

LEGEND

1. GERMAN POLICE HEADQUARTERS
2. BATHHOUSE
3. EMPLOYMENT OFFICE
4. HOSPITAL
5. J.U.S. OFFICE
6. JAIL
7. JEWISH POLICE HEADQUARTERS
8. ORPHANAGE
9. JEWISH COMMUNITY COUNCIL OFFICE
10. MADRITSCH FACTORY
11. OPTIMA FACTORY
12. ISOLATION HOSPITAL

its place a roll of cheap paper. In no time at all and over my objections, the pulleys were replaced by curved hooks or plain nails, which I bent into shape after banging them into the wood. For rope, we used the string that came with the wrapping, which was a lot cheaper if not as strong as the original cord. Dispensing with round rods, Marcel bought flat sticks, and the black paper that rolled up easily was replaced by plain, shiny sheets, which satisfied me as well as the customers but unfortunately disintegrated when handled too much.

Finally, the boss ordered me, when installing the blinds, not to bother with chisels and plaster where a window was topped by a cement strip, but rather to use nails and more nails, which generally snapped off or crumpled. Sometimes the roller was held up by no more than a couple of nails that had somehow managed to penetrate the cement.

I confided my worries to our parents: "All this could have a tragic ending if somebody squeals to the Jewish or German police. If anyone complains about paying a lot of money for the curtains, only to have them fall on his head on his first attempt to use them, it would play right into their hands. They'd be all too happy to get reports of Jewish swindlers producing faulty security products without a license. What's more, if they demanded our nonexistent identity cards, it would be so funny we wouldn't be able to stop laughing."

"What can we do?" Mother said without conviction, trying to calm me. "At least we now have enough bread, and often even potatoes. What can be done at a time like this?"

Father tried to back her up: "The war will soon be over, maybe even before the curtains go bad. Then they'll wind up in the garbage dump anyway." His prediction was only partially fulfilled: The war went on for three more years, but the curtains went out of use in a short while, when the Germans herded us out of the ghetto and into the Plaszow concentration camp.

But I shouldn't jump ahead of my story. Many events were still to occur in this walled Jewish quarter. One of them was of great importance: The manager of the Madritsch factory, which produced military uniforms, placed a large order with us to produce blackout curtains for all the windows of his three-story building, a total of eighty-six curtains. Not to be taken lightly, this order promised to be worth a bundle in money, experience, and prestige.

Marcel brought home the happy news bearing a sack of almost two kilos — more than four pounds — of potatoes, so the whole family could celebrate. He took them out one by one and placed them on the table with a theatrical flourish. "In honor of our unexpected success, in honor of this historic event, we must have a party, a festive dinner." He then placed on top of the rancid, mud-covered potatoes one wrinkled, blackened onion sprouting a pale-green shoot. On each side of this pyramid, which began to tickle our appetite, he set, with another theatrical gesture, a genuine egg, albeit of suspect appearance, and proclaimed loudly, "Tonight we're having potato pancakes. We're going to give Mother a happy surprise."

After my day's work, during which I had equipped four windows with "automatic" blinds, here was Marcel attired as a chef, a paper bag on his head and a wet, dirty shirt tied by the sleeves around his waist. In his hand he wielded a large ladle, and his helper, Iziu, who was similarly dressed, stood by his side. Potato peels covered the floor, and thick smoke irritated my eyes. My two brothers were stirring a dense mixture in a bowl, and the first, experimental pancake was already frying in a pan filled with oil.

"May I taste a piece?" I asked, and without waiting for an answer, I attacked the delicacy with a pair of forks. I was back in prewar days as I stuffed the hot golden dough between my teeth, and perhaps because of the acute burning sensation, or perhaps from hunger, I yelled out, "Delishush! Delishush!"

"Are you crazy, eating food that's still raw?" cried Marcel, as he tried to snatch the searing tidbit clinging to my tongue. But I managed to swallow it anyway. In my stomach it felt like a glowing ember. I bent over and pulled out a large pot from the stack of dishes under the table, and announced, "I'm off to get the soup — we'll have a royal feast tonight!"

I felt my way in the dark street, hardly aware of similar figures moving along the crumbling sidewalk. A gloomy night concealed the despair and overcrowding of the ghetto courtyards. Blacked-out windows hid from view the unfortunate people who were condemned to slaughter and, in spite of all, believed in the coming of the Messiah, which was slated for the nearest future.

It was being said that sages who knew how to interpret the mysteries hidden in the Hebrew letters and writings and could read the stars had learned from the sacred books that a great miracle would occur that year. According to these tomes, the war would end imminently. All sorts of rumors to that effect circulated among the mavens and were eagerly picked up by fine-tuned ears. According to one, a *tzadik* or holy man lived in the ghetto and stood on the roof night and day with a pair of binoculars, searching for a sign from above that would bid him to blow the shofar announcing the coming of the Messiah. Another report had it that the workers in the metal factory had accidentally molded a faucet in the shape of a Star of David. This was a sure sign that the savior would soon bring down the walls of the ghetto and offer a huge loaf of bread to each of the hungry who were now praying for a single stale slice. It was said that the announcer on the clandestine Voice of America radio station promised that a second front would soon be opened and the Allied air forces would annihilate the Nazis and their collaborators with a single massive blow. Soon, perhaps this very night, a shofar would be heard proclaiming from heaven the start of our redemption, the end of the war, and the message that God had relented and revoked his decision to destroy his chosen people.

Breathing heavily, my heart in my throat, I gazed toward the pallid stars and cupped my ear with one hand, lest I miss the slightest sound from far away. However, all I could hear through the thickness of the night was the echoing whistle of a locomotive. Someone opened a window above me, and a yellow light shone from within. Apparently, it was yet another desperate hopeful, who, like myself, expected unreasoningly to hear the holy blast. Meeting with failure, the occupant shut the window in frustration and retreated behind the familiar blackout curtain.

Guided by memory, I crossed more courtyards, feeling my way cautiously in almost total darkness. I kept slipping through fortuitous openings in fences and walls and bypassing stairways of houses that blocked the path. At last, having reached my destination, I took my place at the end of a long line of tired, hungry people armed with a variety of pots, passing the time by guessing at the nature of the soup of the day. The guessing game was an exercise in futility: The acrid smell of beets usually reserved for livestock clearly indicated the kind of slop being ladled out. It was the same soup we had had yesterday, the day before, and a month earlier. Unless the German in charge received the order to liquidate the ghetto, we would be eating the same thin soup two months from now.

My pot filled with broth, I made my way back in a more cheerful mood. Again I walked the uncharted paths, trying to avoid pitfalls, threading my way through gaps in walls and fences, traversing filthy courtyards, and avoiding stairways crammed with discarded furniture. There were no lights and no street signs. Dipping my finger a few times into the only legal food we received, I started to imagine the taste of Marcel's pancakes, soon to complement the fodder beets in the soup. No doubt Mother would bring even more

delicacies for our feast. As I immersed my finger again in the now tepid liquid, I suddenly lost my footing and plunged facedown onto the sidewalk. A vile curse escaped from my mouth as it filled with a mixture of mud and beets. This had to happen just when I was at the door to our house, when I was expecting a delicious meal, above all the pancakes!

Covered with mud and the remains of the soup, I entered the room wearing a silly grin, in acknowledgment that my good intentions had turned sour. Father, Marcel, and Iziu jumped up to welcome me, and their jumbled exclamations confirmed their main concern.

"Did you at least manage to bring the soup?" they asked, as they surveyed my condition.

"What do you mean?" I replied angrily. "Can't you see I've had a terrible accident? What's the matter with you?" I added aggressively, while peeling pieces of beet from the lapels of my jacket. Then I learned the full tragicomedy. The pancakes were ruined. They had been such a success that Marcel had decided to increase the quantity by adding more water and flour. Working in the dark, he picked up a bag similar to the one holding the flour and poured its contents — soap powder — into the pancake batter. In the resulting chaos, the first batch of pancakes, which had been soap-free, were burned to charcoal.

"Well, Mother will surely bring something to eat," I said hopefully, but even this prospect failed to dispel our gloomy mood. I tried to cheer them up with the rosy predictions I'd heard, but a sudden suspicion was gnawing at me. What would happen if Mother came home empty-handed because the guard at the gate became curious about the package that the supposedly dangerous Jewess was trying to smuggle into the ghetto for the enemies of the Reich?

In my frustration, I kicked the pail of coal into a corner behind the clothes cupboard and set in its place the slop pail, which usually stood under the table. Then I asked Father to pour a thin stream of water from the kettle, so I could remove the evidence of my abortive venture from my face and hands. At that moment, Mother came in, carrying a bag of food. She sensed at once, by the light of the flickering candle, that something serious had taken place; the atmosphere in the room was highly charged, even with the electricity cut off.

Before she managed to take it all in, she had to listen to an outpouring of explanations and the stories of our misadventures. She took a deep breath and relieved her shoulder of the heavy load of food. As usual, she made to rest her burden on top of the pail of coal, but of course the slop pail stood in its place. The splash of the dirty water was all but drowned out by our exclamations of horror. This mishap put an end to the festive dinner we had expected that evening.

"Hell, someone gave us the evil eye! Nothing's going well for us tonight!" exclaimed Marcel as he stared at me. "Let's hope that at least the deal we're supposed to be celebrating will turn out better," I said, with a tinge of pathetic hope. We went to sleep on empty stomachs and got up early in the morning with the same empty feeling.

Leaving the ghetto at an inconvenient hour was no cinch. We were embarking on a daring venture to obtain a new roll of black paper. After we had walked some distance from our room, Marcel remembered to tell me that instead of money for an advance payment, he had only a letter to show. I interrupted his confession by asking about the nature of this precious letter, and he explained, "It's from the factory's secretary to the paper distribution office, requesting authorization to buy the roll they require." In order to grasp the situation clearly, I asked him, "Do you think this scrap of toilet paper is going to help us start working?"

"You haven't even seen the letter; and you haven't ever undertaken a major project like this," Marcel yelled back, as he drew from his pocket an envelope encased in heavy cardboard. After wiping two fingers on his coat, he removed delicately, but speedily, a piece of folded paper and gave it to me to read. "Be careful not to dirty or crumple it, God forbid." I understood the handling instructions, but reading the message was beyond my ability. "Nu, do you admit the letter is very impressive?" he demanded.

My first glance encountered the proud symbol of mighty Germany, an eagle clutching a swastika in its talons, its wings spread as if to embrace the whole world. I tried to make sense of the typed text — filled with the usual bombastic Nazi expressions — but with scant success. The document ended with a "Heil Hitler."

"So, how do you like this letter, isn't it worth a pile of money? And you treat it as a joke," said Marcel, as I returned the document to him with an amused expression. "No wonder all you get is pitiful orders with your constant refrain of 'I finished, delivered, and got no payment.'" Derisively, he tried to imitate my voice as he stood with feet apart and hands in his trouser pockets. "In a few days, we'll speak a different language: 'We finished, delivered, and received a lot of money.' You'll see."

Aided by the official letter, Marcel had obtained passes for both of us to leave the ghetto. They were valid for a week, which turned out to be a far from pleasant one. In spite of the dark early-morning hour, crowds of stooped workers in narrowly ranked battalions streamed through the gate, to the tune of the Jewish cops, whose hoarse voices were shouting orders and curses intended to create an atmosphere of fear. Their bestial cries, full of abuse and profanity, drowned out the poor slaves' whispers to each other in a jargon that mingled Polish with Yiddish.

An armed "knight" bearing the Nazi insignia stood like a butcher at an abattoir, isolating those selected to leave this great indifferent world. With the aid of a flashlight, he meticulously counted the passing shadows. As our turn came at last, he boomed over our heads, in a voice smelling of beer and cigarettes, "Two blackout curtains, hop, hop," and we found ourselves on the Aryan side. It was like stepping out of a setting from the Middle Ages into the night of a twentieth-century Inquisition. As the first rays of the sun started to illuminate the sky, blueness spread over church steeples and the roofs of houses that had been cleared of Jews.

The German office where we were headed was at the other end of Krakow, but we weren't allowed to use the streetcars. The sidewalks offered no better alternative for our long walk; there were secret agents and informers aplenty, just waiting to spot a passerby with Jewish features. These petty chiselers and parasites roamed the lanes in order to blackmail any Jews they met for ransom money. Green trucks sniffed out Jews to provide fuel for the crematoriums or to furnish materials used in soap manufacture or as stuffing for mattresses. Armed SS men laid traps to catch Jews for other inhuman purposes: to serve as guinea pigs in the labs, or to work in poison-ridden plants, or to be turned into informers and undercover agents for hunting down fellow Jews. As a matter of fact, anyone was licensed to catch Jews in order to exploit them without pay, or to kill them in whatever manner they desired. Jewish lives had no value.

We walked through this minefield for more than an hour, advancing on a living chessboard where any false move could be our last. Curious glances pursued us. A familiar comment was "Look, they're still alive. Apparently, Hitler hasn't managed to burn all of them yet." Students on their way to school taunted us: "Make way for the officers with the stars," and they pelted us with mud and horse manure or spit in our faces. No one would stand up for us; we could only make a shameful retreat and wipe off the spittle with our sleeves or pieces of newspaper. As we neared our destination, I asked Marcel what he would do if the Germans objected that we'd received a similar permit for paper only a week before. I presumed he wouldn't tell them he had sold it on the black market.

"What do you mean, 'what if'? Don't we have an official letter, with the black eagle, stating that we have a large order that calls for a large quantity of black paper? May their eyes go blind and see only blackness," he said.

"We must have some answers ready; otherwise, we've walked our feet off for nothing, not to mention risking our necks."

"I never prepare my speeches. I'm smart enough to get my ideas during an argument," he boasted, with an odd smile.

At last, we were there. The building was familiar to me, but in my wildest dreams I couldn't have imagined that the old, neglected structure I had known could be transformed, by means of plastic surgery, into such a magnificent edifice. The dirty, peeling walls now bore a coat of yellow paint; the window frames had been redone in gleaming white, and the ancient gateposts were restored. A huge, forbidding black eagle surmounted gilded but austere large Gothic lettering, and the whole front was decked with red streamers bearing swastikas. This insignia explained the magic transformation. Two armed guards in spick-and-span brown uniforms manned the gate, which was flanked by antique stones. Even the flowers, set in the meticulously manicured lawn, seemed to stand up proudly in honor of Nazi grandeur. A steady stream of VIP cars kept crossing the gate, causing the otherwise immobile guards to raise their arms automatically in a Fascist salute, clicking their heels.

To this magnificent edifice the two of us, shabbily dressed Jews marked with crumpled Stars of David, dared to seek entry. Even before Marcel managed to produce the almighty letter in its double wrapping, or to utter a single word, the guards chased us away, as if we were a pair of rabid dogs. Since this wasn't the first time our dignity had been trampled, we didn't complain. Being treated this way had become a part of our nature. However, we still had to find a way to gain entrance.

We approached some Jews who were busy sweeping the sidewalk, and they pointed us to a side door in the courtyard, which was intended for the use of subhumans like ourselves. On the second floor we found a directory, and with great effort we located, among the copious lines of magic inscriptions, PERMITS FOR PAPER ALLOTMENTS.

"Well, here we are," I said to Marcel. "What are you going to say?"

"Everything will turn out fine, you'll see. Just take the letter." He handed it to me and pushed the button at the designated office. I heard a sound of hobnailed boots approaching the door from inside, and my heart started to beat rapidly. A punctiliously dressed, bemedaled German opened the door and screamed, *"Whaaat?"* I waited for Marcel to break the tension with his speech, but when the German repeated his *"Whaaat?"* I understood that my brother had disappeared. With shaking hands, I slipped the letter out of its wrapping and proffered it to the superior being before me. In my innocence, I was hoping that the typed text would excuse me from using my corrupt version of the language of the conquerors.

His Highness reentered the room, with me following. He took a card out of a file and delivered a litany of words, most of which were beyond my comprehension. I assumed he wanted to know what had happened to the permit he had issued only a few days before. He was pointing a fat finger at some entries on the card he pushed in front of my eyes. His roaring seemed to amuse the clerks in the nearby offices, while I tried to get up courage to plead my case. My throat tightened from excitement, and all I was able to spit out were some incoherent words accompanied by facial contortions and violent gestures, without heed for grammar and syntax. In the yapping of my adversary, I could understand only the phrases "Jewish swindlers" and "filthy Jews," which punctuated his fearful tirade. Then he slapped me in the face, first on the right cheek, then on the left. After that, he resumed his seat and filled out a form, which he pushed toward my side of the desk.

In the meantime, Marcel, who had wisely returned outside, carried on a conversation with the Jewish street sweepers. When I joined him, he examined the permit and pompously boasted, "You see, as I told you, they were obliged to give us the permit because the letter I arranged defied refusal."

"What now?" I asked, as we started off in a direction that wasn't quite homeward bound.

Marcel laughed. "What a question! We're on our way to buy the paper, of course."

"Do you have the money?"

"Not even a groschen."

After missing dinner and breakfast, I was too hungry and tired to pursue the questioning. By sheer inertia, I kept walking beside Marcel for half an hour. Then I mustered enough courage to ask, "Have you thought of a way to get the roll of paper to the ghetto? It won't be easy; it must weigh at least two hundred kilos."

"If you think *I'm* going to carry it, you're mistaken. But for the time being, I'm too tired to worry about transportation." He emphasized the last word, in order to convince me that good intentions were all that were required.

"All right, forget about transportation. How are you going to pay for the paper, when you don't have a groschen to your name?"

"Look — first of all, let's see the paper; then we'll worry about payment." He stopped in front of the warehouse and told me to go upstairs with the permit, while he waited outside. Expecting another misadventure, I urged him to come with me. "Are you afraid?" he taunted. "They're not going to beat you here — you're a paying customer. Just make sure they don't steal the permit from you."

A clerk eating a thick slice of buttered bread sat in a small office on the third floor. As he saw me enter, he turned the slice upside down and started to nibble from the other side, hoping I wouldn't see the butter. He read the permit with assumed politeness and a forced smile and informed me that he had just sold the entire stock and the storeroom was empty. I went down to pass on the bad news to Marcel. Before I finished, he grabbed me by the collar and hissed in a loud whisper, "Oh, so the bastard thinks he can cheat us. Run back up and ask his lordship what he did with the roll that was hidden on the left behind the stockroom door. You see, I was there and saw everything."

I did as I was ordered, and the clerk said, with an embarrassed smile, "Please excuse me, mister, I really forgot. This was the last roll

— I'll get it for you right away." Then he started making out a bill and asked me for the money.

"My brother is waiting outside — he'll pay you as soon as he gets the merchandise." I went downstairs to the yard a second time. A man who worked in the storeroom was rolling out the huge cylinder of black paper. He told me my brother had said he'd be right back, that he'd gone to look for a wagon. After a few minutes of anxiety, I was amazed to see a sort of large flatcar drawn by a pair of horses entering the main gate. Marcel sat proudly between the two drivers.

"Marcel, the paper is ready; we just have to pay. Do you have the money?" I called out. To my surprise, I saw him exchange a few words with the drivers, who handed him the required amount. Then he said in a loud voice, "Don't worry, the paper is your security. When we reach the ghetto, you'll receive your dray charges, the loan money, and a handsome bonus as interest."

On the way home, Marcel, seated between the drivers, made them shake with laughter as he plied them with ribald jokes. As for me, I was sitting in the back atop the roll, as if riding a black steed, and beset with gnawing fear and uncertainty. The giant cylinder between my legs was two meters long and weighed about half a ton. Its cannonlike mass kept rolling from side to side, pinching my toes or behaving like a runaway sledge. A few times it almost succeeded in throwing me, threatening to slip down over the unprotected back end and onto the road. I was so inhibited by its evil intentions that I eventually forgot to worry about the money we owed the drivers.

The Madritsch uniform factory was located at the end of the ghetto. Its main entrance was outside the ghetto walls and was guarded with special vigilance. Locked most of the time, it was opened only on special occasions. The Jewish workers, who were paid in tepid soup, entered by way of an improvised path running through the courtyards within the compound. As we approached the gate, Marcel jumped off the wagon, telling the drivers that he was going to open the gate and was leaving the paper and his brother as security. He assured them we'd be through in a minute. Then he merged with workers who were leaving for home.

Time dragged slowly — ten minutes, half an hour — and the gate remained locked. The whirring of sewing machines indicated that the shop was operating, so the gateman must be inside. It would take only a slip of paper to make him open up, so what had happened to Marcel? In the meantime, the drivers stepped down to feed the horses and seemed to be planning their next step, as they threw wolfish glances in my direction and appraising looks at the paper. I saw them counting on their fingers, and one of them rubbed his forehead to make it come up with an idea. The other one whistled loudly and jumped back on the wagon, strategically close to me.

"Mister," he said, with understandable concern, "you *are* acquainted with the one who rode with us, eh?"

"He's my brother. He'll open the gate soon and pay you off." I needed to reassure not only the drivers but myself as well. All sorts of evil thoughts kept crossing my mind, as I sought a reason for Marcel's absence. Had he been detained by the Jewish police during an "action"? Or caught by the Germans without an identity card and sent to Auschwitz? Perhaps they had taken him, along with the other young men, to the new slave labor camp at Plaszow. Where the devil could he be?

Marcel, Marcel, I was thinking, I've always counted on your talent for getting out of tight spots, but this time you tempted fate too much. What's going to happen now? What can I do? My head was bursting with worry, as I remained glued to the precious roll, watching the gate handle for any sign of movement, ready to shout, "Hurray, he's here at last!" But the handle didn't move, while my despair kept growing.

The hum of the sewing machines sent me into a reverie, and I dreamed that I heard the lock turning and saw someone emerging from the gate, but the image dissolved by degrees, until the din of the street returned me to consciousness, in a state of exhaustion and utter apathy. Meanwhile, the roll, with a mind of its own, kept rocking from side to side and pressing its weight on my right foot. By now I was too tired to rest, and even my empty stomach had ceased sending signals of hunger.

"Mister, maybe you should go look for your partner. Maybe he just ran away." I looked up, to find one of the drivers by my side. Wide awake then, I made a move to jump off the wagon and find somewhere to empty my full bladder, before setting out to search for Marcel. But reason prevailed. It dawned on me that they might just want to get rid of me, so they could take the roll to sell on the black market, leaving us without paper or permit. I forced myself to stay where I was.

"What, he's not back yet?" I asked, pretending innocence. Just then, the miracle happened. I rubbed my eyes to make sure I wasn't dreaming again. But no! The gate really opened, and Marcel in the flesh, hale and hearty, emerged from the dark corridor, took hold of the reins, and shouted to the horses, "Viow viow, we're going in!" At last, I was able to leave my perch and go to a corner to relieve myself. Behind my back, I heard Marcel opening a bottle of vodka to celebrate the happy outcome with the drivers. When I turned around, he stood with one foot on the vanquished roll of paper, which had been unloaded, and proffered the almost empty bottle. "Come here, my hero. I left some vodka for you," he said.

"Marcel, where were you? What happened?" I asked, refusing the repeated offer of a drink. "I was so worried about you. Where did you get the money?" After swallowing the bit of vodka he had been saving for me, he said, "It was quite simple. I pawned my permit to leave the ghetto."

To top off the eventful day, Marcel prepared a festive dinner based entirely on fodder beets. The first course was ground beets with vinegar and saccharin; the second, beet soup laced with black flour, oil, and fried onions; and the entrée, beet pancakes made from a mash containing an egg and flour that he fried in oil; for dessert, in place of pineapple pudding, more beets, immersed in a sweetened juice.

After this feast, Dad stifled a burp with his hand and said he was nauseated from all this livestock fodder, but the rest of us licked our fingers and praised Marcel's culinary skill. We discussed at length his exploits of the day. I described my part in getting the black paper, while my brother presented his version. Mom told of her role in the drama: After Marcel had convinced her that the table could still be set without the precious tablecloth Grandmother had embroidered and that there would be no meal without money, she sold that prized possession, along with a few other things, to raise enough cash for food and to redeem the exit permit at a reduced rate of interest. Our dingy room still bore the smell of cooking when Marcel announced that he had to leave us for a short while to run some errand. This turned out to be a gross understatement. . . .

When the hour of the curfew drew close, you could hear rapid steps outside as people hurried to avoid becoming targets for German rifles. Soon the only sound was the measured clank of hobnailed boots worn by the Angels of Death. As always, the blackest of fears assailed us about Marcel's fate. Our imagination worked overtime; we well knew what dangers lurked in the ghetto for us Jews. Then started the recriminations: Why didn't we stop him from going out at this late hour? I knew something was going to happen, because I had a bad dream . . . etc., etc.

Suddenly, heavy steps approached outside the blacked-out window, becoming louder as they descended the hall stairs. "Hell, will no one help me?" called Marcel's voice as he banged on the door. We rose as one from our seats, but before we reached the door it opened wide and we saw . . . a fence being pushed through it. Why a fence? we asked ourselves in disbelief. There it was, made of rough wood covered with mud. Stunned, we watched the monster advance toward the cupboard filled with our last worldly chattels. "Stop, stop," we tried to warn him, but Marcel seemed not to hear. The thing hit the cupboard door with a loud bang, splitting it in

two. At the same time, we heard the sound of broken glass, as our kerosene lamp, which sat atop the cupboard, smashed to the floor, permeating the room with a choking smell and leaving us in total darkness.

"What do you think you're doing? Why did you put out the light?" thundered Marcel, now invisible. We started to search for matches, all yelling at once: "Look what you've done." "Must you always get us in trouble?" In the meantime, I was feeling my way, and my head got stuck between the fence and the doorframe. I spat out at him, "Have you gone crazy with your schemes? There's no room to stick a pin in here, and you want to set up a partition?"

"Partition? Who's making a partition? Have you no imagination, you silly oaf, you damned artist?" Boiling with rage, he tried to enter the room from the other side of the fence. He only succeeded in squeezing me tighter between the doorframe and the rough boards. "I brought some fine lumber to use for the blinds, saving a lot of money, and instead of thanking me you're mouthing insults. Just wait . . . you'll live to kiss my hand for this!"

By the time a flickering candle tried to conquer the darkness, he was inside the room. Lighting another candle, Mom bent over to collect the pieces of glass from the lamp that had fallen bravely in the line of duty. Iziu and I gave first aid to the injured articles among the fallen shelving, while Dad and Marcel pushed the fence back into the hall.

All night long we sweated to dismantle it, pulling out screws and nails that had held the planks together, rain or shine, for many years. "Marcel, where did you get this piece of junk — who gave it to you?" I asked, while extracting the first nail with the pliers. It made a loud squeak, and when I pulled another one from the muddy dry wood, it resisted so much that it bent to a sharp angle.

"Nu, it's no secret: First of all, it's not junk. In the second place, no one gave me this prize material. I just took it when I saw the open door of a shed behind the hospital. I measured the boards by eye and decided they would serve our purpose. Then I returned in the middle of the night and, with great effort, loaded it onto my shoulders and brought it here." He bent over and grabbed the next nail with the pliers, yanking it out.

"There was an idiot guard who, instead of catching the thief, started yelling hysterically, '*Gewalt*, the whole door is running away. The hour of resurrection has come!' Apparently, the shed contained dead bodies waiting for burial. I had no choice but to run with the loot. Luckily, the man couldn't see me in the dark. Nu, here goes another nail."

I looked in awe at the charnel house fence and asked, "Tell me, do you intend to make heavenly gates from this lumber? Do you think I can convert these planks into round rods with the help of a handsaw? You're barking up the wrong tree. They have to be cleaned thoroughly and taken to a well-equipped carpentry shop. That's all there is to it." While talking, I was using the pliers to draw out another rusty nail, which resembled a bloody tooth extracted by a painful operation. Marcel was struggling with one that turned out to be a screw and obstinately resisted being dislodged from the splintered board.

"What's the matter, don't you want to be a carpenter? Maybe I can inspire you with the will to become one, eh?"

"No, my darling brother, I have no talent for that noble trade." I paused briefly to look him in the eyes, trying to guess what his next scheme might be.

We stacked the nailless planks on the floor between the stove and the ruined cabinet, and by morning we had filled three cans that had formerly held sugar, rice, and coffee with nails that could still be used. The floor was covered with dried mud and wood splinters, but Marcel decided that we had to rush off and leave the sweeping to those who used the night for sleeping. I followed his rapid stride, in the speeded-up manner of silent movies. On our shoulders we carried a stack of thirteen boards; every time they leaned to the side, he shouted, "Take it easy, you bastard! Don't you know which leg grows out of the left side of your ass? Left, left, I said." Marcel, though my junior, was quite a bit taller than me. Thus I bore the brunt of the burden. My left hand stretched to reach the top of the boards. It became numb, and I lost all contact with it. The thick dust that rose from the boards with every move produced an attack of sneezing. At first, Marcel wished me "Gesundheit," and I replied with "Thanks," but after a while he didn't react. Suddenly, a splinter started to tickle my ear, and as I tried to remove it with my right hand, another one got stuck under my nail. Without lowering my arm, I tried to pull the sliver out with my numb left hand, but I couldn't find it under the coat of dirt covering my fingers. Not only our hands wore this coating; so did our faces. We looked like chimney sweeps or coal dealers. I was hoping, almost praying, that the guards at the ghetto gate would make us put down our load for a search, so we could get a rest, but on this particular day the Germans were in a good mood and let us cross over, without even asking for our passes. Two filthy guys toting some much-used lumber didn't appear to be a danger to the Nazi regime.

"Left, left . . . Left, straighten them. . . . Can't you hear me, stupid?" I figured Marcel must be feeling even more exhausted than usual, which was why he was venting his anger like this. Some distance from the ghetto, he ordered, "Take off your Star of David." I asked, "Why, is something wrong?" but I obeyed on the run, without argument, and removed the dirty rag. "Where we're going, they don't have to know we're Jews," said Marcel, as he pocketed his own armband. Completely spent, we passed several more streets, and after hitting a building during a dangerous turn, we entered an unfamiliar lane. My left ear, stuffed with dust, heard very little, but my right one heard a key turning in a lock as my brother opened a creaky door. At last, we reached a place where I could sit down on a crate. Marcel relieved me of the dismantled heavenly gate, and I tried to lower my left arm, which was still pointing upward. It retained its threatening posture until I forced it down with my right.

In this tragicomical moment, I perceived, for the first time in my life, a power saw. Marcel showed me how to start and stop it, but neglected to point out the location of a first-aid kit, in case of an accident. He made some adjustments and cut the first slat. It looked to me somewhat thin, but I kept quiet; first, because it would make no difference anymore, and second, because my voice would have been drowned out by the shriek of the saw.

"Well, how do you make round rods?" I asked, though I foresaw the answer.

"You don't. We'll teach the flat ones to roll," he said with finality, while preparing to leave.

"Just a minute — are you finished?" I said, worrying lest he leave me alone in this strange place without some kind of explanation. Marcel wiped his hands with sawdust and said, without looking at me, "I'm going out to buy some nails and rope. I'll be back soon to relieve you, since we have to be finished by noon. You see, this is a barrel factory. The Germans found some explosives here, so the owners can see us only from heaven. That's why we shouldn't be touching anything. A Polish policeman gave me the key as a favor, but for a price, of course. In the afternoon, they'll start demolishing the shop, so we don't have much time. Bye for now, and enjoy your work." Then he was gone.

The terrible noise suppressed my thoughts and feelings. Every time my hands got close to the whirring wheel, I felt as if *I* was getting sawed into strips. I worked without letup, keeping no track of time. The pile of sawdust around me approached my waist. Just as I was finishing the last strip, Marcel walked in. Seeing me in a cloud of dust, unable to hear or speak, sent him into fits of laughter.

In the evening, as I lay in bed with my head swathed in wet towels, while my mother administered all sorts of folk cures, Marcel told me the reason for his merriment. "If you could have seen yourself, you'd have laughed your head off too; I didn't recognize you with your wooden halo, standing in a sea of sawdust. It was so funny I'll remember the sight till the end of my days. It was even funnier than your refrain of 'I finished, delivered, and got no payment.'"

Finally, we started to install the roller curtains in the Madritsch factory. They put at our disposal a small, dank cell, a table with injured legs, and a broken crate for our tools and supplies. The one important thing we did not get was money, not even the agreed-upon down payment of one third. However, this sad fact had no influence on the execution of the order. The manager, who was congenial at the beginning, changed his tune, especially after all the materials had been assembled. While he urged us to work fast, he demanded workmanship exceeding the customary norms. We noticed that whenever the matter of money came up, he became very busy. "Everything will be all right; just finish the work already," he would say.

Marcel assumed that Herr Manager was a true-blue German. However, someone confided to us that he was a German Jew. The truth came out when the work was completed, but then it was too late. We slaved for three weeks, putting in time and effort even beyond what was expected of Jewish workers, from dawn to dusk. We drove ourselves without rest or pity . . . all for nothing! Many unexpected technical snags had to be overcome; we faced moments of despair, when difficulties caused by our inexperience tried to defeat us. We even neglected the individual orders that were our mainstay, and the specter of hunger became our frequent visitor.

With less money available, Marcel had to reduce the expenses. He found that we could save a lot of paper by cutting it in widths, instead of lengthwise; that way we didn't cover any space beyond the height of the window. This turned out to be a fatal mistake. On the night of the test, when Herr Manager and a few other officials checked out the results of our revolutionary invention for blacking out windows during air raids, the building's lights shone as brightly as if the curtains had been rolled up. It transpired that the black paper resisted the change in its nature and refused to sit flat, as desired by Marcel and prescribed by the blackout regulations. The strips bent inward and left a space of several centimeters at the bottom. Our excuses and explanations were to no avail. Not a single member of the testing team believed that such fine, expensive paper had such a tendency to roll. After a war of words with Herr Manager, Marcel yielded and promised that his brother would fix everything. Of course, payment was withheld pending the corrections.

The work turned out to be more complicated than Marcel had indicated to the meticulous manager and his underlings. I had to re-cut every curtain, and to reverse, lengthen, and reglue. Making new ones would have been easier, but we had no choice, as we were out of paper and money. About three weeks from the start of the repairs, I came home just a few minutes before curfew and found everyone asleep. I opened the kitchen larder, and except for two emaciated cockroaches, it was entirely empty. They must have been as hungry as I was, because not a crumb, no potato peel or shred of fodder beet, was to be found. I was hungry enough to eat soap powder, I thought, but its container was also empty. Mother woke up and inquired worriedly who was causing the disturbance.

"It's me, Mom. I'm terribly hungry and tired. Is there anything to eat?"

"We went to bed hungry too. Go to sleep; maybe things will be better tomorrow. Don't waste the candle, it's our last one. I couldn't bring anything today. The custodian chased me out of our store and wouldn't allow me back in to get anything. That's it: I've been expecting this black day and now it has come. Did they pay you anything yet? How will it end?" She finished with a soft moan and wept silently.

"Oh, it will come!" I said, as I put out the candle, letting the darkness hasten the future. Before Mother could reply, a loud knock disturbed the fearful silence. "Who's there?" I asked, in order to gain some time. I knew that even ten locks could not keep out the night callers. Their visits never boded any good.

"Police!" boomed the voice of the Jewish henchman who used to make these nocturnal raids, armed with his whip and a blacklist. At the sound of the voice, I heard the bare feet of my startled family seeking a way to escape in the darkness. They were dropping things, blocking the way to a hopeless exit. "I'm going to —" I didn't finish, as Mother clasped a hand over my mouth and spoke in a whisper: "They've come to check the identity cards." I wanted to say something, but she pushed me down and under the bed. While I was entering this doubtful refuge, I received a knock on my forehead. As I crawled on my stomach, I received another blow; Marcel, who was there already, complained that I'd hit him in the head.

We heard the turning of a key in the lock and the creak of the door. A flashlight beam passed over my face, danced over the floor, and halted on the polished toes of a boot that came to rest near our hideout. Before the policeman stated the purpose of this unexpected visit, before I had time to devise with Marcel some way to extract ourselves from this most dangerous search, I felt compelled to reveal a secret that I had sworn with a solemn handshake to keep forever. I started to say, "Marcel, do you remember . . . ," but my tongue got stuck in my mouth, and I couldn't go on. The secret had to do with Zigo Mahler, who had stayed with us for several months because of an injured leg, which Mother had treated. Several times a week, he was visited by Vuska, Yehuda, and Poldek, and we spoke in whispers so Marcel couldn't hear. Zigo had been shot in the knee during a run-in with the Germans, and he had to remain in hiding. Together with those four, I belonged to a five-man cell of the Akiva underground. My job was to forge papers and official stamps. Obviously, we had been betrayed and they had come to take me away for good. It would be Marcel's job to avenge the death of his heroic brother, I wanted to tell him.

But before my secret could manifest itself in this tense atmosphere, it turned out that we owed the honor of the visit to an entirely different matter. "You used to have a Graphics sign in your window. Is the man still alive?" The voice didn't sound unfriendly, but Mother, expecting a trap, wavered between "yes" or "no." Finally, after a few seconds that seemed like an eternity, she dared to say,

"Yes. What is it about?" My heart pounded, and I imagined Mother's did the same. "Szepesy, the department manager, is looking for a graphic artist. Tell him to pack his equipment and report tomorrow to the secretariat." Without bothering to say good night, the policeman departed, his mission accomplished. After this interruption, we could neither close our eyes again that night nor quit speculating aloud.

"What could it be?" Dad asked, as if he expected us to understand the German mind. "Maybe someone squealed on you because you made a mistake on a sign," said Marcel, trying to scare me. "It could be one of your 'finished, delivered, and got no payment' clients." Mother said, "I think it's a good omen. You'll get a job at the employment bureau, and you'll have unlimited *protekzia* with good pay and lots of food. Everyone there gets a whole loaf of bread to eat by himself at home. I had a feeling that today we'd get some good news, because I had a dream." As usual, she tried to see the rosy side of things, while I worried: They should only not ask for something I can't do.

"When you speak to the manager, offer to sell him roller blinds at half price. I'll give you a commission," joked Marcel. Perhaps he was rekindling his business sense. Iziu came up with another suggestion. "If you're overloaded with work, tell them I could help you cut out the letters and trim the papers."

The prophecies, propositions, and surmises filled out the night. In the morning, I gathered my tools and found that half of them were missing or damaged. Balding brushes were stuck together with dried glue; the compasses were bent; Marcel had marked the spots for screws with my pens, and I found them mixed in with the pliers, the broken hammer, and an assortment of nails and screws; Iziu had used my colored pencils for his games. A few pen nibs were still in good condition, as were a few tubes of watercolors, an eraser, half a bottle of black ink, and the mold-covered drafting board on which Marcel had tried, without success, to make a cake from the infamous beets.

I arrived for my appointment at seven o'clock, hoping to be the first in line. Alas, the office was already working full steam; outside, a line of trucks was being loaded with groups of slave laborers. Every morning, the work crews would be sent to military hospitals and camps to clean the toilets, collect stacks of flea-ridden clothing for delousing, wash the floors, build railroad tracks, haul materials to construct scaffolding, and perform other such menial tasks.

Nazi regulations mandated that every Jewish holder of a *Kennkarte* and an exit pass had to put in a day of forced labor every week in order to stay alive. However, those who had the means to hire a substitute to work in their place for twelve hours in exchange for beatings, soup, and an occasional slice of bread could do so.

As I approached the employment bureau, I was besieged from all sides by eager substitutes offering to go in my place. "Mister, today they're supplying to the quarries. That's not for you. Just give me your *Kennkarte*, and I'll arrange everything." One of them grabbed me by the shirt in his zeal to save me and urged, "Would you let me take your place? You see, Hans, the Angel of Death, is coming for some men, and I happen to know him. The bastard loves to strangle Jews. Nu, just give me your *Kennkarte*. You can pay me when I return it with all the official stamps."

"Many thanks. I have an invitation to speak to the manager about a special job," I said, pointing to my toolbox and drawing board. This aroused their suspicions, and they scattered with fear in their eyes, as if I were infected with a dangerous disease.

The manager's secretary was expecting me. She merely asked if I could draw Gothic letters and maps. As instructed by my mother, I answered every question with *"Jawohl."* If I was wrong, I could

always apologize; in any case, I had nothing to lose. The secretary gave me two slips of paper and said, "This one is for a permit to leave the ghetto. The other is a referral to the German police outside the wall, where they'll put you to work."

At the station house, the police chief launched into a long oration, which I barely understood. Every time he paused, I stood at attention and said *"Jawohl."* After this ceremonial introduction, I was given a few cardboard folders, on which to copy inscriptions from a list. As I started to work, I had difficulty preventing my hands from trembling and struggled to keep the pen steady. The ink in my bottle had become too thick, and the eraser was somewhat dirty. The chief summoned his assistant and both said, *"Alles in Ordnung"* — "It's okay." They lodged me in a little room next to a water closet, which, judging from the marks on the floor, had once contained a bathtub. It was equipped with a chair and a table laden with a large pile of files, which I was to inscribe with titles and numbers.

Toward evening, the chief's aide came in to examine my work and, with a sudden furtive motion, removed from his pocket a package wrapped in newspaper. He put it on the table's edge and indicated that it was for me but I must hide it quickly, so nobody would see it. When I opened the package on the way home, I couldn't believe my eyes. It was apparently the officer's breakfast, consisting of four slices of white bread heavily coated with butter and embellished with fat yellow cheese. I had to overcome an urgent craving to savor at least a few crumbs, to relish the taste that existed only in my memory. Lest temptation win out, I ran home as fast as I could.

My family received me like a conquering hero returning from the front. I had to repeat my summary of the day's events over and over, from beginning to end. After the usual measly evening repast, I placed my package on the table and unwrapped it slowly. The light of candles revealed the rare treasure of buttered bread and cheese, which I divided into equal portions. We ate with smacking tongues, chewing each bite many times. Then we started to reminisce about the food we used to eat before the war. Mom reminded me that I hated boiled beef, chided Marcel about his distaste for tomato soup and Iziu about refusing to eat prune pudding. Dad always complained about the soup being too salty and the meat not tender enough.

"Today you would act differently, eh? Well, the good times may return, but you will have learned to be less fussy, you'll see!" she concluded.

When I finished decorating the police files with their titles, a task vital to the war effort, I started to make door signs indicating the functions of all the rooms in the building. I paid special attention to the importance of the official within: for instance, "Chief Commanding Officer" on the first line, name and rank on the second, and reception hours on the third. Not to be neglected was the red border, whose thickness diminished with the size of the lettering.

After working as a graphic artist for a whole week, I could see some light on the horizon. True, I received no pay, because the Germans placed no value on even the most skilled work of the dispensable Jews, but every day I brought home something good to eat, thanks to the kindhearted deputy officer. He was a strange man, and I never got to know anything about him. When my pass expired, he personally wrote me a work permit valid for a whole year! At the time, it amused me to think he believed the war would last that long, but his permit enabled me to get a *Kennkarte* . . . and the end came after four more years.

Having attained legal status, I mounted a sign on our door in my best Gothic printing. It declared: JOSEF BAU, GRAPHIC ARTIST EMPLOYED BY THE GERMAN POLICE. Now I was entitled to the official food ration, and my fear of being deported as an illegal resident was a thing of the past. Marcel managed to get his lifesaving card in a similar manner. Since his brother was employed by the German police and wasn't able to continue repairing the blackout screens, he was obliged to do it by his honorable self, which now entitled him to a work permit and the identity card.

Indeed, rumors started circulating that the authorities had become liberal in issuing the cards, even to the point of including fugi-

tives from other ghettos, the old and the sick, and the unemployed. This proliferation of the yellow *Kennkarten* was not a good omen.

One day, the deputy officer came into my room and, in place of the usual food package, spread on the table a map of the ghetto and its surroundings. The wall was marked with a black border, and numbers within bizarre circles, squares, and triangles were drawn along the outside. He asked me if I could enlarge the chart to four times its size and deliver ten copies by noon the following day. I agreed, but on condition that I could take the work home, where I had a larger table and a frame for making prints. If I was to meet the deadline, I would have to work all night and the following morning.

"This is a very highly classified document," he said, "but since you're pressed for time, I'm allowing you to take it out of the police compound. However, no one is allowed to see it! Do you understand?"

When I arrived home early, Dad became alarmed until I told him about the classified work that I had to deliver by noon the next day. In the evening, Mom returned in a state of exhaustion from her new job, at the warehouse of confiscated Jewish property. "Congratulations," she said, after pausing to catch her breath. "I'm so glad to see you working again at your drafting table. May this be a happy augury. Is the job important?" I assured her it was very important, because it was for the police, although no money was involved.

"Money isn't everything; it's nice to be busy," she said, stooping to look at the map. Suddenly, I saw fear in her eyes. "Tell me, did they explain why the job was so urgent? There are all sorts of stories about something in the wind," she concluded, in a trembling voice.

"Mom, why is there always something in the wind?" I was tired of her dire predictions, but somehow my own suspicions were aroused by the virus she'd released. "Are you really expecting trouble?" I whispered anxiously. My mind went on a rampage: I saw armed SS men taking up positions in the places marked by numbered circles, squares, and triangles.

"Let's hope it's a false alarm," she said, to allay my fears. "Look, I was lucky enough to get a fresh loaf of bread for myself and another with your and Marcel's ration cards. God willing, things will somehow right themselves." She put the loaves on the table, coughed to clear her throat, and sat down heavily on the bed, to discuss things with Dad in a hushed voice.

The aroma of fresh bread spread through the room and whetted my palate, distracting me from the all-important map. My senses became drunk with the tempting smell. The deadline was approaching, but I was unable to concentrate on my drafting. Mom, seeing my discomfort, cut me a thick, bare slice. The bread's dark-brown hue reminded me of the chocolate tortes filled with nuts and jam that she used to bake for the Sabbath before the war. There were also cakes with raisins and whipped cream topping that used to cling to my nose and chin. They were always my favorites, but their aroma was never as good as that of the sour-tasting black bread that now stuck to my hands and teeth.

Marcel and Iziu came home, tired and dirty after finishing the last roller curtain. "May this be in a blessed hour," said Mom, rapping three times on the wooden table to repel the evil spirits.

"Tomorrow I'm taking a large bag to carry home the money. This time it will be 'finished, delivered, and got paid!'" Saying this, Marcel looked at me for some reaction. "I'm sorry," I told him. "Tomorrow I have to put in a full day's work on a special order, so I can't come with you. It'll have to wait one more day."

"Well, we've been waiting for months, so one more day won't make a difference. Herr Manager promised to pay the whole thing in one shot — for the paper, the other materials, and the work. Oh, we're going to collect a fortune. More money than you've seen in your life. By the way, my work permit expired yesterday, but he promised to renew it for another month, in case some curtains need attention. Just give me your usual blessing, Mom, and everything will go well for us."

"May you always be blessed with success, with God's help," Mother complied. Then she busied herself performing wonders with the available organic matter. By hocus-pocus, she concocted a dish that defied description: too thick for soup, too watery for an entrée. Made of barley, potatoes, fodder beets, and other more or less edibles, it lacked only fat and spices. It served to delude and bloat our stomachs, lest they annoy us with their unreasonable demands. It was Marcel's turn to wash the dishes, which he did while chanting in Hasidic fashion an ode to the meal we'd just finished: "It wasn't very nutritious, was lacking in vitamins and calories, and was hardly filling, but one thing is certain — it's a pleasure to clean up after. No brush or hot water is needed, a cold-water rinse suffices, and don't worry about grease stains."

After the others went to bed, I worked all night, while four candles shed waxy tears for me. Mother talked in her sleep, shouting in German, begging, pleading, and weeping. Dad couldn't nod off and kept tossing and turning. He got up a few times to drink water, scratching the bites of the bedbugs and complaining of heartburn from the lousy food, and he kept asking when I would be finished.

Marcel slept the sleep of the just, with a smile on his face, no doubt in anticipation of the oodles of money he would bring home.

By the light of the sun's first rays, I copied the maps, and the smell of ammonia, which I used to develop the prints, roused the roaches that had fallen asleep after searching in vain for food. At 10 A.M., I delivered the ten copies, but in my haste I forgot the original at home. The deputy officer was pleased with my work and agreed to wait for the original until that afternoon, warning me again not to let anyone see it. "You put in a lot of hours, so you can go home and get some sleep. This is for you," he said, setting a parcel on the table. As he looked at me, sadness and concern filled his face.

Back home, I was about to taste the officer's cake and sausage, when a loud knock on the door brought me to my feet. A Jewish cop entered and shouted in German, "Where is the draftsman?" Frightened out of my wits, I admitted that it was me and asked what was wrong.

"Szepesy, the manager of the employment bureau, wants you at once!" he barked, and made a hasty departure. The usual guard at the office gate had been replaced by a Polish policeman, which was not a good omen. I told him that the manager had summoned me. He admitted me and closed the gate. What the devil could they be planning now? I wondered with apprehension. The clerks in the large office on the main floor were working at top speed. "What's going on?" I asked one whom I knew. He whispered out of the side of his mouth: "They're changing the whole filing system. We've been ordered to list the Jews according to family name instead of place of work, as up to now." I inquired if this meant something was brewing, and he answered in the affirmative.

"So what am I supposed to do?"

"You'll know soon enough; the manager will come and tell you."

I remembered Marcel's invalid work permit. Hurriedly, I wrote him a note: "Marcel, go at once to renew your permit, because tomorrow may be too late. The situation is critical. Joseph." I folded the paper, hoping some passerby on the street would deliver it.

Just then, a hairy hand in the green sleeve of an SS man, who must have crept up behind me, snatched the note as it was about to make an exit through the window. Propelled by two brutal kicks in the behind and a rough shove, I tumbled into the manager's office, only to discover that I had been caught by no other than Wilhelm Kunde, the undisputed master of the ghetto and the foremost enemy of Jews. In ghetto parlance, his name was synonymous with Death. Its mere mention evoked mass hysteria and horror, so he was just referred to as *him* and *he,* after which the superstitious spit a few times to the right and the left.

Now *he* stood before me, his face purple with rage, my note in his hand. "What is this?" he shouted. Aware of what was in store, I resigned myself to my fate; I just hoped not to end my days on this earth by way of butchery.

As Kunde drew his gun, Szepesy, the office manager, jumped up from his seat, slapped me on the face several times, and yelled, "Get out of here, you crazy loon, you maniac!" He grabbed me by the belt, slung me out of the room, and slammed the door shut. My narrow escape from death ended with a somersault and a painful landing under a table covered with file boxes.

"What's the matter with you?" someone next to me whispered. "Don't you know it's forbidden to report about the deportation until tonight's curfew?" When I managed to rise to my feet after a third attempt, the frightened clerks drew away from me as if I were infected with some dread disease. I reached a corner of the room expecting the floor to open up and swallow me, or the ceiling to fall down and bury me in rubble. Standing there, I lost track of time and became numb. The file clerks had already turned on the lights and covered the windows with blackout curtains when a Polish cop came in, and in answer to his question, the clerks pointed me out. He motioned for me to follow. As the clerks watched with compassion, ready to say a final prayer on my behalf, all I could do was manage an indifferent shrug of the shoulders.

Szepesy, Kunde, and two other SS officers waited outside and started marching, with me behind and the Pole bringing up the rear. Many people on the street scattered to hide in doorways or alleys, but those who remained watched the accursed procession, with me in the middle, their eyes wide and mouths agape.

I was sure the bastards were taking me to the main square for a public execution. My heart rose to my throat at the prospect. At least *he* didn't finish me off in private in the office; now I had a chance to inflame the whole ghetto with my death. I tried to compose my last outcry. Should I raise my eyes upward and recite the eternal "Shmah Yisrael," or shout, "For God and Homeland!" or just exclaim, "You dirty sons of bitches, your time will come!" All this prior to my skull being shattered by a bullet. That was the best I could do; but could even the greatest hero come up with better?

Before I could decide on the manner in which I would ascend to heaven, the leading quartet of the parade turned to the right and entered a building with a large open hall. The guard prodded me with his gun to follow. In the hall were several tables, three on each side and one at the end. As Kunde unrolled a sheet of paper on one of them, I saw he was holding a map I had drawn. The building we were in was designated as #1 in a circle. The officers studied the chart and, after a period of deliberation, seemed to arrive at a decision. *He* whistled at me in a manner that could only mean, "Come here, you Jewish dog!" Then he led me around the tables and barked his commands: "Put down here, 'A to C'; this one, 'D to F'; and so on till the end of the alphabet." I had no pencil, no paper except for my *Kennkarte,* so I scratched the letter divisions on it with my fingernail.

Outside, the ghetto was bursting with rumors of deportation. Speculations about the coming horrors spilled into the lanes and traveled from house to house, their wildness forcing the gates of reason. Exaggerated reports passed from trembling mouths to anxious ears until the hour of official confirmation. Everyone heard about my afternoon march through the streets in the company of the SS elite, but now the story grew wings and horns, became inflated beyond all proportion and embroidered to the individual tastes of the teller. When I came home and heard the imaginary details of my meeting with Kunde, I was sure they were talking about someone else, someone who had led the despot through the streets of the ghetto and given him orders to carry out. Our room became the headquarters of a great leader, a master of public relations. Strangers and people who had never deigned to exchange a word with me sat on our bed and on all four of our chairs, seeking my *protekzia,* asking me to intervene with Kunde on their behalf. Undeserved honors were showered upon me, and I was addressed with somewhat insincere respect.

In spite of the strictest prohibition, everyone studied the classified map on my table and became an expert in the meaning of the markings. The noise in the room became unbearable, for everyone spoke at the same time. They kept shifting the candles, spilling wax and leaving their fingerprints on it.

"Please, just mention to Kunde . . ."

"When you speak to Kunde . . ."

"Surely, you can tell Kunde . . ."

In their efforts to arouse my pity, they tried to outshout each other.

"Gentlemen, what is all this about Kunde? What makes you think I can speak to him, that I have any connection with him? I'm

lucky to be alive after he pointed his gun at me." In vain, I tried to tell them the truth, but they refused to let me step down from the pedestal to which they had mistakenly elevated me.

Who knows how it would have ended if we hadn't heard commands being barked outside. "Disperse at once, you bastards! Make way, you damned dogs!" Two Jewish cops entered the room, wielding their weapons — whips, boots for kicking, fists for punching, and foul mouths for cursing. "Everyone out," they ordered. "What are you looking for in here, you dirty whores?" The room having been cleared, one of them turned to me to announce that Mr. Gutter, the head of the Community Council, was here to speak to me. His words took on glorious meaning when that dignitary entered our miserable abode attired in his splendor: a velvet uniform with shining buttons, on his sleeve a red velvet band with his exalted title embroidered in gold. Mr. Gutter, too, was curious about my connection with Kunde and the type of work he had assigned to me. I spilled the whole story and showed him the map and my *Kennkarte,* on which I had scratched the instructions with my nail. "These are the letters I have to prepare for tomorrow morning," I said.

Gutter urged me to use his office at the Jewish police building, where the light was better and there was more room for drawing the signs. "A policeman will come within the hour to escort you. Bring the tools you need, and if you lack anything, just ask me." With this, he strutted out, followed by his honor guard of two policemen. The whole scene had been observed by curiosity seekers, who pressed their noses against the windowpanes, their faces shadowed with a desperate sadness. After the exalted visit of David Gutter, the honorable community leader (may his memory be erased), nobody dared to bother me anymore — I was out of their league.

An hour, two hours, went by, without anyone coming to escort me. As a last resort, I collected a few pages of white paper and my box of instruments and started to walk toward police headquarters in total darkness. Suddenly, I heard a sound, as of a bird flying overhead. I wondered, What kind of bird flies at night — do birds nest at all in the ghetto? Then the sound whizzed closer to my ear; but when I looked around, I couldn't see any flying birds.

When I entered the office of the duty officer, everyone looked at me with astonishment. "How did you get here? Weren't you afraid? They're shooting from all sides. The ghetto is completely surrounded, and tomorrow is the big day. We already have our orders." This disclosure finally revealed to me the real meaning of the night bird sounds.

"I came to draw some signs for Kunde," I said somewhat arrogantly, trying to make an impression. It was an unnecessary gesture, as Gutter had told them all about me. One of the cops politely helped me with my load, another carefully cleaned off the tabletop, and the third apologized for all of them: "We were going to pick you up but were afraid to risk our lives outside. Well, you got here on your own in one piece, but please don't tell on us to Gutter . . . or Kunde."

I went to work with a vengeance. The awareness of our grave situation spurred me on, even though I was totally exhausted. This was my second night without sleep. My worst fears were being realized.

I slipped into a state of semiawareness, during which dream and reality became one. I saw the letters I had drawn rise from the paper and climb the walls, only to scatter throughout the room. Then the room dissolved into a sweet liquid, and I had the eerie feeling that my contact with this evil world, the absurdities of the ghetto, and the signs auguring the coming calamity merely a constituted bad nightmare. I saw myself lying in bed in our prewar house, waiting for the alarm clock to wake me for school . . . but it wouldn't ring. After procrastinating for what seemed like an hour, I rose and opened the window to get some fresh air, but the tension-charged

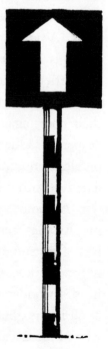

70

atmosphere and the odor of the night preceding the "action" choked my lungs. I tried to refresh my face with water from the tap, but it came out warm, sticky . . . and red.

Though the drowsiness clung to me, I returned to my table and resumed the signmaking. My head was exploding with pain, and as I cradled it with paint-stained hands, I again found myself in our old apartment. It was a sunny morning. A bag filled with notebooks containing my homework and school textbooks covered in paper waited for me on a chair. The aroma of sweet coffee and fresh rolls invited me to the living room for breakfast.

"Mommy, Mommy, I had such a terrible dream. We were locked up in the ghetto — do you know what that is? It's something from the past, but it's not possible now. Yet I dreamed it was happening. Jews, thousands of Jews, stood in a square, surrounded by soldiers who kept shooting at them. There were piles and piles of dead bodies, with rivers of blood flowing from them . . . and a mighty wail arose from these mounds and remained hanging in the air . . . and I was running between the bullets and the cries of the dead. Mommy, I'm afraid this dream will become real." Then my mother placed a hand on my shoulder and said in a male voice, "But you must finish your work; it's almost morning. How about it?" The response came from one of the policemen, who was shaking me by the shoulder: "You still have lots of work, and you're sleeping, eh?"

At 6 A.M., on my way to the center of the "action" in the hall with the seven tables, I stopped off at home, showed them the seven signs I had finished, and asked for their *Kennkarten*. "I hope to get some *protekzia*. At the least, I'll get the blue slips for all of us," I said with conviction, as if to confirm that there was some truth in the stories about my connection with Kunde.

In the hall, everything was ready. The SS men sat behind the tables and the Jewish cops stood beside them, while Kunde issued his final orders. Then he helped hang the signs, and the ingenious apparatus for grinding up the Jews was set in motion at full steam.

I was first in line; I stood before an SS brute under the A to C sign. When I handed him all our *Kennkarten*, Kunde whispered something in his ear. I thought the boss must be telling him that I was the man who had sat up all night to draft these pretty signs, so I and my family rated the *Blauscheinen*. However, the whisper was apparently of an opposite nature; instead of attaching the all-important blue slips, the fat hand that was holding our cards tossed them into a drawer and pointed to the door.

The person behind me shoved me aside to take my place. Then the Jewish policeman kicked me in the rear and shouted, "Get a move on, you bastard, you're in the way. Get the hell out of here." Before my mind could take in my own and my family's situation, another Jewish cop dragged me to the door and, with the aid of a German, threw me down the stairs, where a large group of the Special Brigade *(Sonderkommando)* was waiting. A *Kennkarte* with a blue slip entitled the bearer to exit to the street, but anyone deprived of it passed into the hands of this unit. I still had not yet absorbed the meaning of my predicament when the Specials started to play volleyball with me. The last in the line gave me a punch in the belly, and I passed through the gate to the courtyard in reverse.

Two SS men were in charge of the courtyard. It was their job to receive those who, either because they lacked work permits or because their skills were no longer needed by the Nazi regime, failed the fateful test. By order of the mayor, all these "idlers" were deported to the concentration camps, where they became more productive. In those days, as I said, we still didn't know or didn't want to know that the transports led straight to the crematoriums. We wouldn't believe that the Germans, known to the enlightened world as "bearers of culture," were capable of planning and carrying out, in cold blood, without pity, the mass destruction of human beings by industrial means, as if they were bedbugs, flies, or other pests to be exterminated. By that time, we knew well enough from our personal experience and that of other Jews that the Germans could be brutal murderers and sadists. However, in our wildest imaginings, we couldn't picture the special ovens for burning human beings. Prior to the war, we had heard of crematories for incinerating the remains of people who didn't want to be buried, but the herding of living men, women, and children into gas chambers and the burning of the corpses. . . . And to have this happen on a daily basis, to bring in fresh transports without respite, to make soap from human fat and stuff mattresses with people's hair, to extract gold teeth and sell the clothing of the slain — this was beyond the ability of the normal mind to absorb. No, whoever was spreading these macabre stories had to be either demented or a provocateur trying to foment a riot that would incite the Germans to wipe out the ghetto.

The two SS men whose job was to guard the candidates for transport and to arrange them in perfect rows even resembled ordinary soldiers carrying out an unpleasant task unwillingly. When one SS man pulled one of my maps from his pocket, in order to explain something to his buddy, I screwed up enough courage to try telling him that it was I who had drawn it. Perhaps . . . But when I started to break ranks, an SS man who resembled a human being grabbed me by the hair, dragged me toward the wall, and beat my head against the bars of a window. I became dizzy and fell to the ground, so this presumed human being abandoned me for dead and went on to administer similar treatment to someone else. I heard shots, screams, and pleas for mercy. Fear imbued me with new strength, and I managed to crawl on all fours back to my place in line. Suddenly, like the blowing of the shofar at the end of Yom Kippur prayers, a voice rang out: *"Achtung!"* — "Attention!" The line of people whom God had abandoned and whose fate it was to quit this world within a few hours was seized with panic. We were marched forward, without knowing why or where. Then I recalled drawing on the map the number 2 in a circle in the courtyard of the Optima factory. We left through a side entrance, tightly hemmed in by a detail of SS men holding their fingers on the triggers of their guns and seeking a suitable target on which to spill their loads. I was the first in line and saw that the sidewalks were already filled with endless rows of the pious moving slowly toward the Inquisition. They must have covered all the streets of the ghetto. A few of my acquaintances sent me looks of compassionate irony, which could be read as "See you in the transport." I answered with a shrug of helplessness.

Now I could see that my mother had been right in predicting a black future; the Germans were following the map. The Optima factory had once produced chocolate, and the yard had been left intentionally large to allow for future expansion. Now that the world had turned upside down, the courtyard had become the center of black-market activities, with bread serving as the medium of exchange. The chocolate factory had gone bankrupt — the palates of the conquered were less selective and more easily satisfied with basic foods, without regard to taste. Just something to put in the mouth was enough, never mind calories or vitamins. With eating a necessity, instead of a pleasure, chocolate was out of the question. On the other hand, the most popular product among the Nazis was army uniforms. For that reason, the Optima market, which was accused of trading in optimism, had to engage in distributing the official garb of the world conquerors. Not unlike Madritsch, it pampered the knights of the swastika with uniforms that inspired fear and terror, as they still do in my memory today.

It goes without saying that when I was tossed into the Optima yard, my thoughts were far from recalling the history of the building that had once housed the chocolate factory. My primary desire was for sleep. Not particularly convenient, but after a couple of days of nerve-racking labor on an empty stomach, after the severe beatings and humiliation, I longed to sleep, even if for a few minutes, even while standing. So as soon as the guards yelled "Sit down," I collapsed on the weed-covered ground. But my dreams refused to take wing, having lost their power to tranquilize me.

As more deportees flowed in, the yard became crowded. Like me, my fellow prisoners weren't aware that the Nazis were merely deluding them with the story of work camps. Like me, they refused to believe that we already had an appointment at the Majdanek abattoir, that we were at a way station on our final journey. Like me, they believed that after a while, at the latest by the end of the war, we would return to our homes. In spite of this, we wished to avoid the transport, out of an instinctive dread of the unknown.

Millions of wise, intelligent Jews, whose brilliant minds could cope with any situation, paid with their lives for believing the greatest lie in humanity's annals. The only thing that might be said in their favor is that the truth was so preposterous, so impossible, that even history, which doesn't record many new things under the sun, had no precedent in all its texts for a deed of this magnitude.

Like millions of other European Jews, we too, in our little segment of the Holocaust, just a few thousand of us, awaited our fate. Each with his own private suffering, each trying to find some *protekzia*. We stayed down because standing up was punishable by summary execution on the bloodstained grass and sand. Men, women, and children crawled on all fours or slid on their bellies in order to find a place closer to the fence. The air was charged with tension and filled with the dry-throat noises of desperate people looking for ways to save themselves. Each one believed in a personal miracle that would return him to the familiar area of the ghetto. Each was concerned only with himself, having no mind for anyone else.

"Guten Appetit!"

As for me, I had no plans for the immediate future. Every road to salvation was closed. My brain was drained of ideas, and I sat silently among similarly afflicted men and women, in whose faces I could see the reflection of my own fears. In my reverie, a curtain descended on the macabre scene, and when it lifted, the place was empty and the pogrom atmosphere was gone, along with the stench of sweat and urine and the whistling of bullets. I felt a strange detachment from the events of the day. Mom was standing beside me, tendering a package wrapped in one of the maps I had made for the police.

"I brought you some hot beet soup; you must be very hungry."

"But, Mom, why did you go and ruin the map? I have to deliver it to the deputy first thing in the morning. What's going to happen then? The whole thing is crumpled! Why did you have to wrap the soup in my map? Was there no other paper in the house?" I tried to salvage it, but when I grabbed hold of the paper, I heard a voice calling me in the distance: "Bau! Bau!" Mother set the package on the grass and asked, "Can't you hear that you're being paged?" She cupped her ear in order to hear better. "They're calling you again. Why don't you answer — are you deaf?"

The voice was coming closer, very close. I wanted to stand up to ask who was calling and for what, but my rear stayed glued to the ground and fear stilled my mouth. "Bau! . . . Bau!" The voice was now in front of me, but I couldn't see its owner. "What's the matter with you? The man who was looking for you went away, and you didn't even answer him." Mother bent down and started to unwrap the map. She took out a plate and filled it with hot borscht. I extended my hand for the dinner, and Mother came closer. "What's the matter, are you ashamed of your father's name?" With that, she emptied the bowl in my face.

I awoke covered with perspiration. Again I saw the teeming, excited crowd around me and felt the heat of the sun. The air was full of German curses and shouts, whistling bullets, and the cries of dying mothers and babies. The rising souls of the martyrs were staging a protest in heaven. I slept and no one woke me up, because there were already many corpses waiting to be buried.

Once more, I heard the voice calling for me in the yard: "Bau! Bau!" Was I still dreaming? I looked around and spotted a Jewish policeman walking away, still shouting my name. Mustering all my remaining strength, I crawled forward on my knees and yelled like a madman, "I'm here, I'm here!" I clambered over the bodies, collided with crawlers heading in the opposite direction, trampled dead children, and screamed until my voice became hoarse: "I'm heeere! I'm heeere!" I tore off my shirt and started waving it in the air. My knees were bloody, but I kept after the cop, who by now had stopped calling my name. "I'm here, sir, here I am, sir." A few bullets, apparently aimed at me, whistled by and missed their target, hitting someone else. Bereft of strength, I clung to the boots of the policeman when I reached him. "Sir, here I am."

When I had caught my breath, I found myself lying on the sidewalk outside the yard. In front of me, a line of victims streamed through the gate of the Optima, to be sacrificed on the altar of racial hatred. The bloodthirsty SS men shouted, kicked, and shot into the procession of Jews on their final journey.

The policeman helped me to my feet. "Mr. Gutter arranged with the German authorities to return all your family's *Kennkarten*, together with the blue slips. Your mother picked up the others already. Hurry home, because they're waiting for you and it's dangerous to be seen on the streets. Hold up your card so everyone can see it."

I don't remember if I kissed the cop or only thanked him profusely, but I will never forget the walk home. Death had not completed its harvest. The Nazis and their devoted agents, the Jewish police, were searching every house in the ghetto for people lacking *Kennkarten* and the blue slip. Those caught had to pack a few be-

longings hastily and make a run to the transports, but the SS men on the street made sure that neither the runners nor the luggage made it to the Optima. The Nazis abused every victim before claiming his soul, which was doubtless already en route to its Creator to lodge a formal complaint. The abandoned bodies covered the pavement with blood, waiting in vain for the tears of their families and the prayers for the dead. The bags filled with their last worldly goods were now the property of the Reich.

Holding the *Kennkarte* over my head, I proceeded through the SS men and Jewish cops engaged in hunting human prey. I picked my way among the slain and their bundles and between the flying bullets. Only when I was home and found my whole family sitting on the bed, bemoaning my fate, was I able to relax. As I crashed in, there was a mutual outburst of joy. Everyone had to touch me, to make sure I was really alive. Mom embraced me, looked in my eyes, and exclaimed, "I still can't believe it!" Then her lips moved in silent prayer. Dad drew the blackout curtains and said, "On so mournful a day, it's not becoming to display such happiness." Then Mom lit two candles, and it was a moot question whether she wanted some light or wished to celebrate our survival.

Suddenly, I looked at my drawing table and saw the map I had copied for the police; it lay there crumpled and torn, just as it had been in my dream. "Who spoiled the map?" I asked. Mom answered, as if she were still part of my vision, "You must have grown deaf from happiness. I've been trying to tell you, but you're not hearing me."

When we finally calmed down, she gave a full account of the events of that historic day. Friends had come to tell them the terrible news of my detention, but they were unable to leave the apartment for want of *Kennkarten.* To be caught outside without that document meant certain death. My family was trapped. Someone even suggested they pack their bags and join the transports. As a last resort, Mother came up with a brilliant idea. She took the map, decorated as it was with the symbols of Nazi Germany, and went to try her luck, hoping *this* document would open every door. All she had to say was that her son had created it, and the officials involved in the expulsion of the Jews would come to her aid. As it turned out, however, the map failed to influence the conscience of the Nazis. Disappointed, she walked home, folding and unfolding the map, which had proved so impotent. By chance, she met Gutter, and in her despair she reminded him of his former offer of help. She explained the whole situation, and the head of the Jewish Council, who generally didn't excel in kindness, took the map and went with her to the office of the German authorities, where they granted his request. Poor tired and injured map — it was you who saved us!

Marcel went the next morning to Madritsch to collect the money, but he came back at once: Herr Manager had been taken to the transport. It turned out that he had only pretended to be a manager. In truth, he was just a go-between, dealing with the real management. Marcel learned that this man had received the money long ago, and his informants were surprised to hear that he'd kept it all for himself.

"Well, there's nothing to be done," Marcel told us. "The goddamn manager took the money, and the goddamn Germans took *him.*" Then Marcel removed the roller curtain sign from the window.

I chided him. "Does this mean it happened to *you* this time: 'I finished, delivered, and . . . ?'"

"And they didn't pay me," Marcel conceded. Then he added, "Don't despair. Tomorrow we're starting work on a new invention. Lots of people are being moved to the Plaszow work camp, and they're allowed only to take a blanket and pillow with them. . . . I have a brilliant idea: it's possible to remove some of the stuffing from the pillow and convert it, by means of a special stitch, into a comforter. I'll get right to work on a new sign. Meanwhile, you can take your inks and paints and the map from the drafting table and make the top level. In a few days, people will be lining up to order the ultramodern Supercomforters."

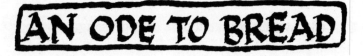

AN ODE TO BREAD

Flour hardened to a loaf of concrete
as payment for one day's torture.
Behold the loaf!
Eight empty bellies, staring through the eyes,
carve up the prize
into eight equal portions
with no crumb wasted.
Behold the idol!
To him we address
our most ardent thoughts,
from behind these triple layers
of walls, mighty barriers
of electrified barbed wire.

And I, one of eight to share this loaf,
grateful owner of a slice spread with the memory
of abundance and fullness (may they rest in peace),
I beat my breast and beg you,
Forgive my past insults, uttered so thoughtlessly
in times of plenty.
Forget my unjust words to loaves before the flood,
when I called them "heavier than lead,
dry as wood, tasteless, hard to digest."
False charges all!
Forgive me, kind bread,
my heresies against the sacred loaves
I squeezed on grocery shelves, saying,

"Dough's half raw, not fresh enough, unappetizing,"
words fallen from an ignorant tongue.

To all the loaves of wheat bread, rye bread, dark bread,
enriched with a layer of butter or jam,
which were demeaned, rejected, forgotten,
till the insults made them dry up
or hide beneath a skin of mold
to be tossed into a garbage dump,
I say:

Kind bread, forgive me and the other hungry millions,
whose empty stomachs shamefully confess their sins.

THE SCAFFOLD

A s ghetto dwellers, we tallied up the many variations of suffering and torture we could expect and came to the erroneous conclusion that the cruel inventiveness of the Germans had reached the point of exhaustion. In our innocence, we thought they could not imagine any more sadistic, sophisticated methods of inflicting suffering and that no human being could stand additional or harder blows. We were convinced that more harshness would either kill the victims or drive them mad. Soon, though, our delusions were shattered; we underestimated not only the Germans' talents but our own stamina and ability to endure abuse, which exceeded even the estimates of our masters.

In comparison to the conditions that prevailed in the concentration camps, our ghetto life had been a nest of beneficent luxury. At least in outward appearance, we resembled ordinary people; we dressed normally, if not exactly in accord with the latest styles, and we dwelled in rooms that, though not very comfortable, offered fairly reasonable conditions. We lived as family units, albeit reduced in size by the war. In other words, we retained a measure of humanity. It could not be said that we enjoyed personal rights and security or that we could attain some standard befitting the twentieth century, yet between the "actions" and the random murders, we still managed somehow to exist. Having a key in one's pocket was a symbol of minimal privacy.

In the camps, we became an open target for all sorts of barbaric perversions of the bloodthirsty beasts. There we were just one of a group; we worked, slept, and ate together, just as we washed, undressed, used the toilets, and copulated in front of strangers. All the same, each of us remained a solitary, lonely unit within the crowd.

In the ghetto, we had had control over the water supply; we had watches by which to tell the time and calendars to count the seasons. The German newspapers, if read between the lines, brought news of the world, and people who worked outside the walls brought us up to date on the local scene. In the camp, however, the sound of a trumpet took the place of a timepiece, and only the color of the sky, together with other signs of nature, helped us to determine, roughly, the months and seasons of the year. As a result, it is almost impossible to fix with any accuracy the dates and hours of important events.

In general, we described the time informally by stating, It happened some time ago . . . one night . . . in the daytime . . . before the morning roll call *(Appell)* . . . during the evening roll call. We would also add the season: It happened during our first/second/third summer . . . in the winter/spring/autumn. . . .

During the first autumn, the Germans announced one evening that it was forbidden to leave the barracks that night, to undress, or to go to sleep. This was accompanied by the usual warning: "Offenders will be executed at once."

Obviously, something was about to happen, and the rumors started to fly. So-called eyewitnesses spread "true reports" from reliable sources: The Nazis are in full retreat on all fronts; their lines of defense collapsed with the first attack by the Allied forces; all the camps close to the front lines have been liberated, and thousands have gained their freedom. . . . The Russians are advancing rapidly, and their main objective is the concentration camps, so they can liberate the tortured inmates. . . . In the areas they've already conquered, they're distributing millions of loaves of bread to feed the hungry. . . . The British have opened a second front, and camp inmates have been mobilized to execute the captured Germans, one by one. . . . Rommel has been defeated in Africa, and the French under de Gaulle are advancing toward Italy. . . . The Americans have flattened every city in Germany; Berlin has been wiped off the map. . . . Mussolini has defected and is asking the Russians for asylum. . . . Hitler has surrendered unconditionally. . . . All Nazi government buildings are flying the white flag.

The authors of these heartening reports added in conclusion that "our" Germans were very tense and likely to run for home in the middle of the night, because they were ashamed for us to see them flee. . . . This was it; the war was ending at last, and if all went well, we would be free before daybreak.

I looked out the window and saw the watchtower lights scanning the camp, as if nothing was happening. Slowly, they swept the grounds around the electrified barbed-wire fence, and I saw by their glow groups of guards making their rounds with their dogs. Well, obviously the news hadn't reached them yet. The traffic on the road surrounding the camp was the same as usual — a few vehicles drove at leisure in each direction. Not a single convoy of military forces, no excitement.

All this looked very suspicious. One by one, the lights went out in the free houses outside the wall. The frogs croaked a prayer to the smiling moon, and someone was playing a distorted version of a popular song on a harmonica. There was no sign of any unusual happening that might confirm the rumors. Once in a while, we heard hoarse voices, the sound of hobnailed boots, and random shots. This was very strange — could it be that not everyone had heard the news? Were we the first to know? Perhaps the Germans themselves were spreading the stories in order to have an excuse to wipe out the camp this very night.

In my excitement earlier, I had swallowed more than the usual nightly portion of margarine-covered bread. It must have been midnight by then, and I was again feeling the pangs of hunger and thirst. I cast about for a drink of water, but my fellow inmates were waving their empty bottles in the air. They had drunk to the last drop the filthy liquid that had lain idle in our fire buckets for months, and our fire corner had become a public lavatory, a local branch of the camp latrine.

A feeling of uncertainty gradually overshadowed the rosy predictions, and fear resumed its usual place. Everyone was pacing impatiently, speaking in excited tones and watching the entrance. The barracks elder stood by the door, whip in hand and anger in his eyes. To every inquiry he had but one answer: "Leave me alone. I'm thirsty too, and I need to go to the toilet. Are you looking for a bullet in the head? If so, just try going outside." And if anyone did try, he was rewarded with a kick in the behind and a vile curse. Then he had to take his place in the line to the fire corner.

The adjoining hut was experiencing the same fear of the unknown. There, too, people paced the floor, lest their exhaustion, their inability to sleep, get them in trouble. Their elder was likewise not averse to using his whip. Their frightened patter and guessing games about the intentions of the Germans were just as futile as ours.

At dawn, an SS man burst into our barracks and ended our speculations. His uniform was spick-and-span, his boots were highly polished, his cap was decorated with the skull and cross-bones, and he wielded a whip and a gun.

"Line up, you stinking Jews, line up!" he bellowed.

I didn't know where I was supposed to stand, as everyone was running around in a panic. The aisle between the bunks, which was normally narrow for even one person, suddenly became wide enough for two lines. To add to the chaos, men kept climbing down from the upper levels. Someone grabbed my shoulders and pushed me forward; someone else grabbed me by the throat and shouted, "Get back, back, let me pass." All of a sudden, a shaved head emerged between us from below and a hand started feeling my face. There was no room for me to lift an arm in self-defense.

A shot reverberated, followed by a mad scream, which made us turn, as if electrified, in a single direction. In my haste, I stepped on somebody, who let out a moan, and my feet got tangled in some rags. For a second, I lost my balance, but I kept running with the others, without pity, without regard for anybody, without knowing where. Beneath a shower of blows, we somehow managed to form single lines in the aisles. The SS man was shouting angrily: "God-damn dogs! Filthy Jews!" Near me stood a pale individual, his eyes wide with fear, trying to pull up his pants but managing only to in-sert both legs in one side while mumbling, "He wouldn't let me fin-ish my shit. What could I do? He wouldn't let me finish. . . ."

In our confusion, we didn't notice the two men who came in with a bucket of red paint, which they placed next to the first fellow in the line before starting to work on him from both sides with their brushes. They painted epaulets on his shoulders, then lines around his belly and both sleeves and, in large numerals, his personal number plus a Star of David on the chest. The pants were marked with stripes of the kind worn by generals, but the knees were circled with thick bands. The painters worked rapidly, without uttering a word or paying heed to the body within the garments. The SS man stood with feet apart, moving the handle of his whip in rhythm to his bellowing: "One two, one two, one two!" When they finished daubing zebra stripes on a man, the Nazi gave him a mighty kick that sent him flying to the other end of the barracks.

The daubers were generous with their paint and had no regard for neatness. Their work done, they hoisted the bucket and proceeded to the next hut, to do the same to the men there. My neck and hands were spotted red, and I felt this aromatic, sticky redness soak into my skin, creep into my body, and mix with my blood.

When the Nazi passed the fire station corner, he halted, covered his nose with a hand, and let out a terrifying howl. Then he grabbed the four nearest men by the collars and ordered them to empty the buckets at the latrine building. After an hour or so, they came back with the same pails, filled with the black water that was known in our camp lingo as coffee. The thirsty inmates lifted the pails like giant mugs and gulped down the liquid. The four bearers cried out in disgust, "Pigs! Don't drink this filthy coffee — can't you smell it?" Then they told the hut elder, and anyone else willing to listen, how they had emptied the pails into the latrines but weren't able to wash them because the water was shut off. Using pull, they asked in the kitchen for some water to rinse the pails, but all they got was this coffee, which hadn't been boiled. For want of a place to dispose of the filthy liquid, they brought it back to the fire corner.

I was among the first to quench my thirst with the drink, taking large gulps and holding my breath as I dipped my face in the pail. This saved me from looking at it too long and inhaling the stench. Meanwhile, other thirsty men kept pulling at the pail from all sides, and I felt the foul liquid dripping down my neck and chest and into my trousers. When I finally had enough and withdrew my head, two others squeezed themselves into the opening. As I wiped my face with my sleeve, I felt something sharp scratching my skin. To my surprise, it turned out to be the red paint, which by then had dried.

A trumpet blast announced the start of the workday. The darkened lanes filled up with tired men who had spent a tense, sleepless night. From then on, we would be marked with the red stripes, which detracted even more from our erstwhile appearance as human beings.

On the mustering grounds *(Appellplatz)*, I met my brother Marcel, who worked now in the upholstery shop. He gave me a mysterious smile and whispered in my ear, "Want to see something funny? Come with me." Without waiting for an answer, he pushed me back into a circle of light coming from a window, put his hands in his pockets, and thrust out his stomach. "You see, I fooled them!" Then he demonstrated his new creation — he had dipped his striped outfit in red dye, which made the stripes almost invisible. He told me to do the same, but I refused.

The sun was late in coming and, when it did, was half asleep, as if still considering whether to start the new day. Heavy clouds hovered over the camp, making it difficult for even the most ardent prayers to reach the heavens. It was wet and cold; our wooden clogs filled with mud, which also clung to our freshly decorated clothing, covered the worktables and walls, obscured the view, invaded our thoughts, and drowned our hopes. On such a morning, one became indifferent to one's surroundings. Like all "good" news in the past, any rosy tidings we may have entertained the night before were conspicuous by their absence, with no apology. They seemed likely to absent themselves in the future too.

Generally, in this accursed, grim space, surrounded by barbed

wire courtesy of the Germans, only the blackest predictions of the certified pessimists had any chance of becoming bleak facts. The war, still unsated, demanded new victims every day. We feared that by the time peace broke out, no one would remain alive to enjoy it. Our immediate vicinity gave scant encouragement, and there was no hint over the clandestine radio that the free world was aware of the degradation of our living and dead, or of the death factories operated by the Nazis. Nor was there any sign from above that the Master of the Universe had been informed of the contempt shown His Honor. The feeling of impotence, of being thrown to the dogs, stifled any daring ambitions, froze any heroic plans before they could hatch, and created a general indifference to our fate at the hands of the oppressors.

My work consisted of drawing plans for the construction office. The job was not physically taxing, but it was still possible for me to fall at any time in the line of duty. One was as likely to receive twenty blows on the buttocks as a whiplash to the face, a bullet to cure a headache, or all of these together. There was no apparent reason for these punishments — they were simply a form of the Nazis' entertainment. Occasions for receiving a passport to the next world presented themselves hundreds of times daily.

The Germans, especially in such weather, used to send us to work outside the camp on special tasks such as hauling stones, piling wood, or digging graves. I was lucky that day to be detailed to the office of an SS officer just beyond the gate. I was ordered to paint signs in the following vein: ALL THE WHEELS ARE TURNING TOWARD VICTORY! . . . THE JEW IS YOUR ENEMY! . . . JEWS, LICE, TYPHUS, PLAGUES! Still, I was in a warm, bright room, seated on a normal chair at a normal table. Gradually, I started to feel more human, which gave me hope for a better future. I slipped into a state of reverie. I was the owner of a drafting office and was treated with respect by everyone. Then I said, "So long, fellows," and went outside because I felt like it. Where did I go? To a restaurant, so I could eat and eat, with the fat running down my chin. I ate . . . and ate . . . and ate. . . .

Then, during this imagined feast, I looked out the window. On a hill across from me, the site of the Jewish cemetery of Plaszow, encompassed by the camp, I saw men hard at work, busily smashing the headstones. One of them, wearing a red suit, stood leaning idly on his sledgehammer. I recognized Marcel.

I asked the German in charge to give me a pass, so I could go to the warehouse for paper. With the aid of this form, stamped with the black eagle, I crossed all the gates and entered the area of the former cemetery. Marcel, still leaning on the sledgehammer, told me with a smile that all upholsterers had been sent that day to smash the headstones and turn them into gravel to pave the camp's roads.

"Look how the sons are desecrating the resting places of their fathers. Do you think the souls who left their dry bones under these crushed stones are now busy lodging a complaint with the Almighty? You're waiting for a miraculous intervention from above, are you?" Saying this, he kicked a piece of white marble, picked it up, and read the inscription, while regarding me with contempt. "Here, take it as a souvenir, a reward for your faithful service to Mr. Hitler." On this fragment of a tombstone dedicated to someone named, perhaps, Grossbau or Sternbaum, only the letters of our family name remained, BAU.

After a moment's silence, Marcel smiled again, in an effort to soften his words. He took my hand and put it against his red trousers: "Can you feel it? I fooled those supermen. I found five gold cups hidden in one of the monuments. They took away four of them, but I managed to keep one. It's worth a fortune — we'll be rich yet!"

With difficulty, I managed to overcome my shock and said, "Marcel, I think it's better to return the cup to the Germans. Why

look for trouble? Besides, I came to tell you that the red suit makes you stand out among the others, and if you don't work, you'll get a bullet in the head." In reply, he smiled once more and traced a few circles on his forehead. "What? Me work for the Germans? You know that isn't my style!"

I went back to painting slogans. I could still see the people on the hill crushing the tombstones into gravel for the road. The sound of the sledgehammers pounded in my ears in an irregular rhythm. Marcel was no longer to be seen among the workers.

Evening came, to end another day of suffering. Dense smoke, emitting the smell of burned flesh, rose above the barracks and signaled that this was the last night for the camp's latest dead. They departed in the form of white smoke, rose easily upward, waved their hands in parting, and viewed with pity all those who remained behind. Then they danced gaily in celebration of their new freedom, before disintegrating in the air.

I kept making signs, ignoring their text and intent. Famished, I

waited eagerly for the approaching hour for our daily rations, at that time a kilo — slightly over two pounds — of bread for every six people and a package of margarine for each dozen. With Marcel, I planned to visit Mother, who worked outside the camp and occasionally brought us something good to eat, such as potatoes boiled in their skins, pieces of dried bread, or white beets. I was looking forward to sitting on her bunk and hearing the latest news — she always bore good tidings. Lately, she had promised that very soon we would have peace and freedom, that we would return to our apartment and eat fat, juicy chops and other meats. Each one of us would get a whole loaf of bread, without having to worry about to-morrow. . . . In my skepticism, I tried to visualize how she would look in a dress painted with red stripes, consistent with the latest fashion.

A knock on the door disturbed my cogitations. In came a Jew-ish Kapo in his neat uniform and shiny boots, a whip in his hand. "Perhaps you know where I can find some rope?" he asked. He spoke with a politeness that befitted my temporary place of work. "I was told there's a bundle of heavy rope in this room; would you know where it is?"

"This is my first time here, but I'll help you look." I opened a cabinet, pulled out drawers, got down on my knees to check under-neath, but found nothing. "What's the rope for?" I asked, while searching in vain under another cabinet.

The Kapo started to lose patience. "Didn't you hear? There's going to be a swinging party tonight on the parade grounds. Every-thing's ready and they're supposed to start in fifteen minutes, but suddenly I discovered we're out of rope."

"I've been working here all day, and nobody told me a thing." I was standing on a chair, feeling with my hand between two crates on top of the cabinet. "Do you know who the unfortunate candi-date is?"

"They caught a young guy today who stole some gold." The Kapo thought telling me his name would make me hurry. "I forget what they call him — something starting with *B* . . . Ba- or Bi-, something like that."

I stood on the chair, turned to stone, with my hand stuck between the two crates. The room became dim, and the furniture started to wheel around me faster and faster with a mounting shriek. The Kapo was turning together with the furniture, and he shouted something at me. His voice tried, without success, to surmount the ringing in my ears. With exaggerated caution, I stepped down from the chair, trying to ward off a flock of black crows, a symbol of doubt and hesitation. I sat down heavily, and my head drew me forward, eyes fixed on the face of the hangman. My weightless arms swung to and fro. The hangman, like a predatory fish, kept closing and opening his mouth. All at once, my dizziness was gone, as he jumped toward me and opened the drawer of the table. With a cry of triumph, he pulled out a bundle of flaxen rope. Slamming the drawer shut, he upset two bottles of ink that were on the tabletop. One was open, and the red ink ruined the poster I had been working on. I remained glued to my seat as the Kapo left hurriedly, tying a noose. The red ink spread over the white sheet and eradicated the word "Juden," which I had drawn just before the entrance of the hangman.

I was at a loss for ideas. It was too late to save my brother now. No amount of pull could help. In desperation, I asked the manager of the office to excuse me from the *Appell*. I told him about the spilled ink, which meant that I had to start the poster over, but it wouldn't take me too long. As was usual in such cases, he started to yell, accusing all Jews of irresponsibility and a negative attitude toward work. In the end, he telephoned the duty officer and told him that prisoner number 69084 had to complete a very important job and would return to camp only after the assembly. The man at the other end of the line apparently consented and said something that made the manager laugh uproariously. Raising his arm, he ended the conversation with "Heil Hitler."

A trumpet blared in the distance. A floodlight came on over the entrance to the camp, and the barrier was lifted to admit the groups of prisoners returning from their workshops. They started to march toward the parade grounds, where my brother must have been standing in his red suit, barefoot and without his usual smile, waiting by the scaffold. His hands were bound with a wire; there were shiners around his eyes and a bloody scab on his forehead. He was probably hoping for a last-minute miracle, perhaps thinking I

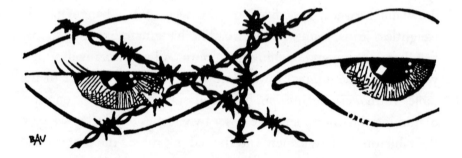

would intervene with the Germans and beg for pity. Perhaps he was concentrating his wits on a plan to escape....

I felt a pressure in my throat; something damp covered my cheeks and my mouth tasted salty. Oh, Marcel, Marcel, so you fooled the supermen. You did it well; it couldn't have been done better.... As the tears ran down my face, the sharp Gothic letters became a slippery, trembling mishmash. After another hour of voluntary overtime, I collected all the slogans, compared them with the original text to spot errors, and handed the lot to the SS officer, who gave me leave to go "home."

At the camp gate, I reported that prisoner number 69084 was returning from his job at the office. The SS men, skulls and crossbones on their hats, gazed at me without interest as I entered the barracks quarter. I walked slowly into the night, with my clogs scraping over the fresh fragments of marble, which only that morning had been converted from tombstones into gravel. I ventured alone through the wrecked cemetery, between broken monuments covered with mud. I was alone now. Marcel and I had always been together, even if we hurt each other once in a while. Perhaps I had beat him up without reason, perhaps I'd insulted him at times. . . . Now, on this terrible night, I beat my breast in atonement, as the wind seemed to recite the Kaddish, the prayer for the dead, over the violated graves. In the moonlight, I could see the tatter of a tallith, a prayer shawl, fluttering on the barbed wire, while a rain of teardrops descended slowly on my face.

I didn't notice that I had passed the parade grounds, passed the scaffold, and reached the barracks. The noise and the lights brought me back to reality. It seemed that everyone was looking at me with compassion. I thought people were shunning me in order to avoid having to offer consolation or answer questions. I passed the men's barracks with a lowered head and, without uttering a word, entered the women's barracks. Mother, wearing her black kerchief, welcomed me as always. Kissing her, I avoided looking into her eyes. She pulled the muddy clogs from her swollen feet, hung her leggings on a nail, and sat down on her bunk. She told me that her group had worked hard outside the camp and returned after the roll call. She had just come in and hadn't even managed to empty the bag of food she had brought. She already knew what had taken place during the assembly and wondered why Marcel wasn't here yet. I didn't explain the connection between the victim of the day and her son.

Life was proceeding as usual, as if nothing had happened, as if it were normal that Marcel went today and it would be someone else's turn tomorrow. The day before yesterday they killed five people, and yesterday all the sick ones went to the incinerator. There were more than twenty thousand Jews in the camp, and the killers were at the ready. Nobody approached Mother and me, but it was evident that we were the center of attention, a place accorded the families of those who had perished.

Mother unwrapped half a loaf of bread from its wrinkled paper and started preparing our supper. Three margarine-topped slices, each covered with a third of a hard-boiled egg and a slice of onion, appeared on a lace tablecloth that had seen better days. "This is a surprise. Marcel will be very happy — he loves boiled eggs," she said. My throat choked with sorrow, as if held in a noose. I told Mother that because of a headache I had suffered from all day, I had no appetite. "I just came to see you, Mommy, and wish you good night," I lied. With a parting kiss, I ran out, fearing my eyes would betray me.

Outside the upholstery hut, a crowd was engaged in vigorous trading, like in a real market. The sellers roamed impatiently, whispering instead of hawking their goods aloud: "Cigarettes . . . cigarettes . . . Who has saccharin? . . . Who wants salt . . . tobacco . . . three lumps of sugar for a cigarette?" One held an egg on the palm of his hand, as if to remind people who had forgotten what one looked like, and intoned, "Hard-boiled egg . . . hard-boiled egg . . ." I pushed my way through the hawkers and buyers and entered the dirty, smoke-filled hut. The floor was covered with a carpet of mud, and smelly, wet rags were hanging between the beds. Emaciated, tired men sat on the triple-tier bunks, like caged animals in a zoo. I was looking for Marcel's friends, who would tell me the whole story. Suddenly, I was accosted by the barracks elder. "Are you looking for Marcel? I just saw him go out to arrange something. Wait, he'll be back in a minute."

My ruined world suffered another tremor. I didn't know whether I had lost consciousness or the man was making fun of me. But the living proof of his words, wearing his red suit and a sarcastic smile, shouted at me from a distance: "You see, I did fool the supermen! Luckily, I didn't listen to you. The gold is already sold and I'm loaded!" He took out a fat bundle of German money from his pocket, while I watched him with wonder and joy.

When I returned to my hut, I was told that the Germans had hanged a boy named Beim. He had been employed in the storeroom for valuables, and during a search, they had found a gold watch in his pocket.

WALL OF DESPAIR

They stand rooted in the earth, transfixed in the black soil,
mocking our helplessness with a metal-fanged smile:

Pillars, pillars, abandoned by the sun,
affixed with barbed wire to our walls of despair.
In the silent evening they do not sleep,
and not in the depth of night, but stand in ambush,
their lethal knife held at the ready.

Beyond the deadly wires,
where sobs are generated by the gusting winds,
beyond the wires, which drip with bloody rust
and hone their sharp nails, drunk with electric charges,
Freedom prances. . . .
Look! as she unwraps a buttered slice of white bread
. . . and gorges on it to the last crumb.

Far from the tangle of wire, there is still,
so they say, a sane world that we, destined to die
from bullets sprayed from the watchtowers,
know nothing about.
Already our foreheads are marked with a red circle,
to make it easier for the snipers to aim.

T he death camps were an integral part of the Nazi regime, from its very conception to its inglorious downfall. Electrified barbed-wire fences, watchtowers sniffing for human prey, dense clouds of smoke, which reeked with the smell of burning flesh and adhered to the striped uniforms of the inmates — nothing will erase these images from the memories of the survivors among those who were caught up in the diabolically conceived, perfectly executed Holocaust machine created by Adolf Hitler and Associates.

For six million Jews, those years of total madness became their terminal years; for the small number who lived through it, who managed by some miracle to smuggle their souls through the various "actions" and selections, this devastating period left scars they have carried and will carry for the rest of their lives. No amount of German reparations and subsidized holidays at health resorts can make them forget.

The years of my youth were a ransom paid to history for the dubious privilege of witnessing and participating in this, the most macabre epoch in Jewish annals. The story of the concentration camps is like the scenario of a horror movie directed by someone devoid of human emotions, whose purpose is to scare the audience and to set its nerves on edge. How can I now convince those without understanding that these shocking events really took place, when I myself find them beyond human comprehension? When the Germans started the last stage of their Final Solution in the summer of 1942, the Jews were already sealed hermetically in the ghettos, stripped of all rights and property, and thoroughly brainwashed against any thought of resistance. Then the Reich extorted from them the final payment — their lives.

The Nazis chose an appropriate place for implementing the genocide of the Krakow Jews, their new cemetery in Plaszow, on the outskirts of the city. As a start, by means of forced labor, they desecrated the fresh graves by erecting upon them the first of many huts or barracks and placed there a misleading sign, WORK CAMP. After herding the Jews from all the ghettos in the area into the cemetery, they unveiled the true purpose of the place with the sign CONCENTRATION CAMP.

The camp didn't arouse misgivings at first; a few residential huts, a kitchen, a bakery, latrines, and workshops were not cause for panic. But soon it became obvious that this was the prototype of a death camp, with all the facilities required for mass murder. The facility was expanded well beyond the cemetery, to encompass surrounding lands and houses within a radius of four kilometers.

After their defeat, as they retreated in confusion, the Germans found time to obliterate the camp entirely; they burned the tens of thousands of scattered bodies and dismantled the incriminating huts before carrying them away. Later, the Poles placed a memorial on this historic site, but except for the cemetery, the annexed lands were returned to their original owners.

Lest its existence fade into oblivion, I shall try to reconstruct

Plaszow from the shards embedded in my consciousness, to construct a model of this veritable hell on earth. I owe it to the countless camp inmates, those who died there and those who will carry its imprint on their souls to the end of their existence.

I will now take you on a guided tour of my model. We'll start with the main gate, which today has been obstructed with a barricade. To the right, you see the train tracks and two station buildings (202, 203). The hapless victims were shipped from here to the furnaces of Auschwitz or to other camps, to work in factories producing the implements that would enable the master race to conquer the world.

When the Kapos — the Jewish supervisors appointed by the Germans — ordered the locksmiths to install barbed-wire grilles in the doorways of the railroad cars stationed on the tracks, we knew that an "action" was imminent. Rumors started flying from hut to hut, and the dread of new agonies joined the fears that were our daily fare. All hopes of even a partial redemption were long gone, but the thought of being transferred to a strange, uncertain destination made matters worse.

Since there were no clocks or calendars in the camp, time dragged on slowly toward infinity. At indefinite intervals, the freight trains laden with human cargo departed. No one expected to hear from the unfortunates again. The barbed-wire fences shut out effectively any communication with the outside. When it became known that the locksmiths had commenced their work, the inmates started planning how to survive the anticipated selection. All means to this end were justified. Young, prematurely gray men blackened their hair with pieces of burned cork and reddened their sunken cheeks with the dye from paper wrappers of chicory. Those who had money bribed the servants and clerks of the Germans and concealed their remaining valuables within the intimate recesses of their bodies. An open market existed for helpful information or to provide protection

from the evil. Thus the privileged whispered about there being some well-guarded secrets to survival, but no two versions were alike. It was pathetic to see how members of families who were forced to separate did so without any display of emotion, as their tear ducts had dried up long before. The air of uncertainty gave an added resonance to the horrors that were the order of the day.

Through this gate, countless thousands arrayed in rows of three shuffled their wooden clogs to the monotonous "Left, left, left" rasped hoarsely by the Kapo. The barrier lifted above the shaven heads of the marchers, their only crime indicated by the word *Jude* stamped on their identity cards. A bitter slogan was born in the camp: "You enter here through the gate — you exit through the chimney." How near the truth!

We are at the start of the twentieth-century version of the Via Dolorosa, four kilometers long and lined on both sides by a three-meter-high electrified fence, powered by high-tension wires strung between porcelain terminals. Along the outer rim of this wall of death lies a complex arrangement of barbed-wire coils five meters wide. Thirteen watchtowers perch over the whole system, each of them heavily fortified and equipped with machine-guns, telephones, and constantly revolving searchlights. The towers are manned by SS guards day and night, while unleashed dogs, trained to attack people in striped suits, roam the area. This formidable complex, designed to preclude any attempt at escape, was constructed by the forced labor of the inmates under the supervision of the Germans, according to plans that had been pretested for efficiency in other camps.

Today the gate is unguarded. Nobody searches us for concealed bread or sugar. There is no Kapo to announce in a loud bellow, "Twenty-two prisoners from the building detail." Our next stop is the domain of the Angel of Death and his faithful helpers, the armed SS battalion and the police chief. Even the sun feared to

enter this forbidden area. Some say it failed to get a pass from the authorities.

Today the law of the jungle no longer applies. We can walk in respectful silence, as befits a sacred place. While our shoes tread over the gravel, listen, please, to the language of the stones: They are weeping, and when you lift one, you feel the texture of marble. These are not ordinary stones; they bear Hebrew inscriptions. Yes, the Plaszow roads were paved with the fragments of elegant monuments, which the prisoners were forced to crush and scatter over their surfaces. Under these stones, squeezed down into the earth by heavy rollers, is buried the cemetery itself.

Now we are passing two important buildings. On the left is a two-story house (155) built before the war, which served as the headquarters of the duty officer and contained the telephone exchange and a radio transmitter linked to a series of loudspeakers. During the "actions," they broadcast dance music to the entire camp. On May 14 (one of the special dates impressed on the prisoners), for example, the Nazi operators amused themselves by playing a German lullaby, "Good night, Mommy," while a transport of children and sick people was being dispatched to the Auschwitz crematoriums.

On the opposite side of the road stands the headquarters of the camp commandant (201). His name was Amon Goeth, and he was a hideous, fat monster weighing more than one hundred fifty kilos (three hundred thirty pounds) and standing more than six feet six inches in height. His reputation for depravity terrified the population, causing them to shiver in fear and their teeth to chatter. His cruelty defied human comprehension. Using tortures surpassing anything known to the Inquisition and with terrifying capriciousness, he dispatched his victims to their eternity. For the slightest infraction of his rules, he would pummel a hapless prisoner's face and watch with sadistic pleasure as it spit broken teeth and became swollen and blue, the eyes forced from their sockets. When administering a whipping, he compelled the victim to count the lashes and, if in his agony he made a mistake, to start counting again from the beginning. During so-called interrogations, the accused was hung by the feet from a hook in the ceiling of Goeth's office and a dog was sicced on him. When someone escaped from the camp, his group was lined up in a row and told to count off by tens. Then Goeth would personally execute every tenth man.

At one morning *Appell*, he decided to have some fun. Accusing a Jew of being too tall, he shot him and proceeded to urinate on his still stirring body. Turning to the man's shocked friend, he yelled, "You don't like this, eh?" Then he killed him as well and urinated on him. There was the case of a hungry man who stole a potato from the storeroom. Goeth had him hanged near the gate to the prisoners' quarters with a potato stuck in his mouth and a sign proclaiming, "I am a potato thief." Once, he caught a boy who was suffering from diarrhea and was unable to contain himself. He forced the boy to eat all of the excrement before killing him. Every morning, after a meal of raw meat mixed with fresh blood, the mad commandant would tour the barracks in the company of two fierce bulldogs that had been trained to tear people apart. After such visits, the hut

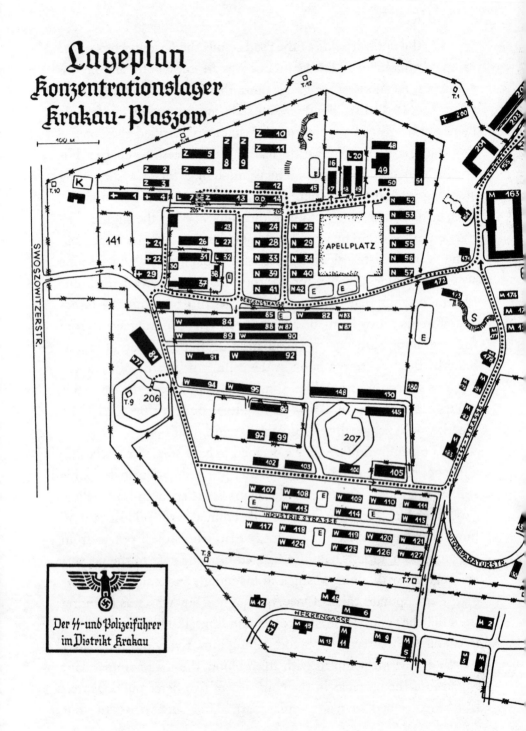

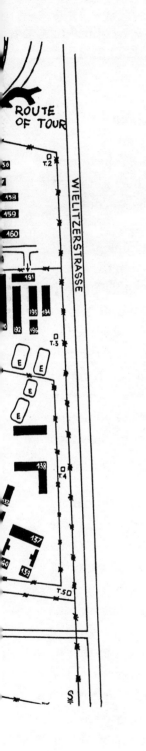

ROUTE OF TOUR

WIELITZERSTRASSE

LEGEND

Z	WOMEN'S BARRACKS
N	MEN'S BARRACKS
W	WORKSHOPS
M	GERMAN DWELLINGS
T	HOSPITALS
L	LATRINES
K	SITE OF CREMATORIUM
E	WATER POOLS
T	WATCHTOWERS
S	STONE QUARRIES
1, 4	ISOLATION WARDS
14	JEWISH POLICE (ORDNUNG DIENST)
18, 19	QUARANTINE (KAMP QUARANTÄNE)
20	QUARANTINE LATRINE
21, 22	INFIRMARY
23	LAUNDRY
27, 32	CENTRAL LATRINE
30	MEAT STORES
31	FOOD STORES
37	KITCHEN
38	BAKERY
48	CLOTHING DEPOT
49	BATH HOUSE
50	DELOUSING STATION
77	BRUSH BRISTLES STORAGE
81	POTATO STORES
82	SHOEMAKERS
83	WATCHMAKERS
84	LOCKSMITHS AND TINSMITHS
85, 88, 195	CENTRAL STORAGE
87	ELECTRICIANS
89	FOUNDRY
90	PAPER PRODUCTS
91, 94	CARPENTERS
92	PRINTING SHOP
95	BRUSH FACTORY
107, 108, 113, 117, 118, 124	TAILORS
111, 115, 121, 125, 126, 127	MADRITSCH CLOTHING FACTORY
114, 119	FURRIERS
120	UPHOLSTERERS
130, 131	CHEMICAL LAB
132	GARAGE
133, 134	BOOK STOREHOUSES
137	PIGSTIES
138	STABLES AND CARRIAGE HOUSE
139	RABBIT HUTCHES
140	POULTRY BARN
155	TELEPHONE EXCHANGE
163	GUARDS' QUARTERS
164	"GRAVES HALL"
171	GRAY HOUSE
172	ADMINISTRATION
173	BROTHEL
176	NCOS' HUT
177, 179, 181, 182, 183	OFFICERS' VILLAS
178	RED VILLA (GOETH'S RESIDENCE)
180	KENNELS
200	GERMAN HOSPITAL
201	HEADQUARTERS (SITE OF CONSTRUCTION OFFICE)
202, 203	RAILROAD STATION
204	MAIN GATE
205	GATE TO WOMEN'S CAMP
206	GORKA CHUJOWA
207	MASS GRAVE

inmates tallied the result: fifteen to zero, twenty to zero, thirty to zero. The zero was always on our side. We could have killed the monster, but we knew the score then would be twenty-four thousand to one.

The headquarters also housed the construction office. There Jewish engineers had to perform sometimes crazy assignments at a frenzied pace. No matter how impossible their mission, they managed to carry out projects that no trained engineer in his right mind would undertake. They labored without relief in order to complete the assigned quotas, which kept increasing all the time.

An engineer named Greenberg was in charge of implementing the commandant's schemes. Any delay or error resulted in the severest of punishments. Greenberg knew that the chief couldn't afford to kill him, so he habitually owned up to the errors of others, who would otherwise have suffered a bullet to the head. He absorbed in silence blows that would have felled a boxing champion. After this abuse, Greenberg would no longer resemble a human being, but he was forced to continue working, without medical attention or even first aid. In my Plaszow, I place an eternal flame above the commandant's hut, under a sign reading: IN SACRED MEMORY OF SIGMUND GREENBERG, WHO SACRIFICED HIMSELF TO SAVE OTHERS. GRATEFULLY REMEMBERED BY THE PLASZOW PRISONERS.

For a while, I worked in the construction office as a draftsman. My task was to draw a map of the camp. On more than one occasion I underwent the official punishment of "twenty across the ass," and it took a few miracles to save me from certain death. As a result, I lived in constant fear of Commandant Goeth. My nerves were so frazzled that it was enough to hear his voice, even muted by a closed door or from a distance, for my face to drain of the last drop of blood. When he was in the vicinity, or when someone said that he was on the way, I became pale, my lips felt icy, my heart stopped beating, and my spine felt like a nest of ants. I would be left with a headache that lasted for hours. One time, clerks from the other rooms entered my office to warn me that Goeth had arrived and there was a good chance he would come to my desk. I shriveled up inside and, overwhelmed by visions of death, awaited the fateful arrival. When these warnings became a frequent occurrence, Greenberg consoled me with the following advice: "First of all, Goeth hasn't been in the camp for two weeks. Second, they're making fun of you, because all they have to do is say he's coming for you to act like the wonder of the century and turn white as a sheet. They're only too glad to demonstrate the phenomenon to any skeptics."

We're approaching the site of "Graves Hall" (164), the ruins of a fashionable building that had originally served as a funeral parlor. The Germans converted it into a stable. When the number of horses they pilfered from the Jews reached a hundred, they transferred them to another camp and blew up the building. For some strange reason, the walls were only partially demolished. Could they have been kept to serve as a symbol of the degradation of Polish Jewry?

We'll now turn left toward the guards' barracks (163). This rectangular single-story house sits adjacent to a broad courtyard surrounded by the huts of the Ukrainian militia, a kitchen and a mess hall, a canteen, the workshops of Jewish tailors and cobblers, and an arsenal. To add to the gloomy atmosphere, the gate to the barracks was adorned with a forbidding tower, reminiscent of the Middle Ages.

I remember when we erected this military compound. It was during a winter of icy winds blowing sheets of sleet. The location was a sloping street covered with muddy soil. Dozens of Jews died slaving to put up this edifice. Carpenters, plumbers, and tinsmiths had to work day and night without respite. Others were detailed from their usual tasks to carry building materials. Between the morning and evening roll calls, they formed a constant parade coming and going, their shoulders burdened with planks, pipes, stones,

and bricks. One time, a wagon filled with rocks collided with a large column supporting a part of the building, causing it to collapse like a deck of cards. The SS man in charge, named Huyar, blamed the building manager, Dinah Raiter, for the mishap and started to shower her with heavy blows. Mercifully, the small, frail woman fainted, but the brute kept beating her with sadistic pleasure, until the body was smashed to pieces. I heard the sound of the whip as it cut the air and saw his red face rising and falling over the pile of bones, rags, and blood. Still not satisfied, he fired a volley of bullets at what used to be a woman, as if to make sure she'd never rise again.

We proceed now to the Gray House (171), which was built before the war. The notorious thugs Huyar, Zdrojewski, Eckert, and Glaser resided here. The basement served as a prison, equipped with all the trappings of a chamber of horrors. There was a narrow iron cell, just big enough for a man to stand in but not to lie down, which could be sealed hermetically. Another cell was horizontal, of a size sufficient for shoving a prone person in headfirst, as in a grave. Other refinements included a whipping bench, chains for hanging a prisoner, and heavy leather whips made from dried-up bulls' genitalia. Completing the installation were dark, dank isolation chambers with only a small opening for water. Very few who passed through this institution exited under their own power. They had to be dragged by the legs straight to the grave, next to the others who had been murdered the same day.

The intersection we've come to branches on the left to the New District, where the villas of the officers (177, 179, 181, 182, 183) and the Red Villa of Commandant Goeth (178) are situated. As we turn right, we approach the stone quarries lying at the foot of a hill. All the camps contained quarries, but the one at Plaszow was something special! Here women hauled wagons of rocks to the New District, where SS Strasse begins. The Germans called it, ironically, the Manpower Train. It consisted of three wagons joined together, each holding two tons of stone. Seventy emaciated women, arranged in two rows, were hitched to the lead to do the work of a locomotive. They were dressed in rags or sacks and grossly undernourished. During a twelve-hour shift, they had to fulfill a quota of fifteen trips, regardless of darkness, icy cold, pouring rain, snow, and mud.

The work of crushing the boulders was done by the punishment detail, whose members had their backs marked with a red circle. Theirs was the most arduous labor. The man in charge of the quarry was a German of pure Aryan stock, whose chest was marked with a green triangle denoting a professional criminal, of which he was proud. His greatest pleasure was murder. When no other victims were available, he would pick on the Jews. He boasted of being a graduate of the Dillinger gang in the United States, which had won him a life sentence. He loved to knock down a victim and strangle him by slapping a rod across his throat and pressing it with his feet on either end. Another of his so-called games was to order someone from the detail to carry a large rock on his back and run in a circle, while he stood in the middle and rained whiplashes on him as if he were an animal in a circus. This lasted until the victim fell down and was crushed to death under the boulder. As the one in charge, this criminal invented his own refinements of the various ways to kill and insisted on carrying them out personally.

Adjacent to the quarry is the brothel (173), which served the SS personnel. Because of the racial laws, no Jewesses were employed here. Closer to the road lies the administration hut (172). A detailed index of all prisoners was kept here. Jewish clerks were forced to compile lists of the sick, the old, children, and those who refused to work; all were destined for the crematoriums. By way of contrast, the clerks also compiled lists of food and other kitchen supplies. Daily reports of the morning assemblies at the mustering grounds and a list of the barracks elders were also posted here. In the yard of this building stood the scaffold.

One winter, the construction office manager had an argument with the camp administrator. In order to spite him, he decided to use me as the butt of a joke. I was working with a group of electricians at the time. He ordered me to come to the construction office and to stay there, without worrying about the roll call, as he had arranged everything. It turned out that he "neglected" to arrange anything and had failed to notify the Kapo of the electricians that I was with him. Later that night, Greenberg reported to the officer at the gate, "Twenty-two prisoners of the building detail and one

electrician." As a result, I was reported missing during the evening roll call, and for several hours they searched for me all over the camp.

On account of me, all the prisoners were forced to remain standing in the snow, and they missed their meal and rest period. I was told of this as the administrator rained dozens of lashes of the whip on my head. When he was finished flogging me, he made me thank him politely, ask for forgiveness, and promise never to do it again. Barely conscious, I rejoined the building detail for the return to the barracks. The building manager later boasted of his coup against the administrator.

As we pass through the inner gate, we enter a camp within a camp. Here the huts of the living quarters are surrounded by fences that mark off the various subdivisions. There is a camp for men, another for women, one for Poles, and a few smaller ones, all with barbed-wire enclosures. Each camp had its own guard, and anyone entering or leaving in the line of duty had to stand before him at attention, cap in hand, and state his request in a loud voice for His Eminence: "Prisoner number 69084 has a duty to perform at such and such a place and requests permission to pass." Every hut had its own elder, and each camp division had a Kapo. Both "dignitaries" had to give their permission in turn.

Dear visitors, we are now approaching the mustering grounds or *Appellplatz*, where the roll calls were held. On this broad expanse twenty-four thousand people assembled twice daily. Under ordinary circumstances, this number of people could have filled a medium-sized city. For us, roll call sometimes meant standing an entire day — twenty-four hours — without respite, without food, forbidden to speak or to go to the latrine. God help anyone who uttered a word, moved out of line, or tried to sit down! Some managed to sleep standing up, some wet their pants when they were unable to contain themselves, and nobody knew what next lay in store.

On regular days, we stood here at six o'clock in the morning, arranged by various work details, lined up in threes by the Kapo, who reported to the SS man on duty the number of fit prisoners, the number of the sick who were given permission to stay in the barracks, and the number of deaths that had occurred during the night, the corpses to be handed over to the "heaven detail."

On the other side of the square were the men who had finished their night shift. They were grouped according to their huts, and the elder reported with precision the number of prisoners who had survived the rigors of the work and the number of bodies brought back on stretchers. At six in the evening, the process was reversed. The SS men checked the reports and counted the assembled; if there was a discrepancy, we would remain standing until the unfortunate who was still asleep in his bunk or had joined another group without reporting was found.

Between Bergenstrasse and the mustering square, you can see two pools of algae-coated water. After a series of fires, the commandant ordered the demolition of the small huts, which stood too close to each other, and the erection of larger ones from the salvaged materials, to be spaced fifteen meters apart. A fire brigade was organized, and fifteen of these pools were dug but never used. Instead, they formed a perfect breeding ground for mosquitoes. This was an addition to the lice, bedbugs, and fleas that afflicted the inmates.

The next street passes between two rows of the men's barracks (N). Each hut is divided into two sections by a long corridor. The two sections are long halls lined by rows of pallets from floor to ceiling. Next to the door facing north are the fire extinguisher and a big pail of water. In the middle of the hut stands a small heater for winter use. There are no closets or shelves, because the inmates own no private property, apart from their personal bugs. There is a nail on the side of the bunk; people would argue about the right to hang a rag on it. Other items, such as a dish and spoon, the wooden clogs,

caps and shoulder bags, were rolled up for the night in the striped uniforms and served as pillows. All were the property of the SS authorities but had to be safeguarded against theft by their temporary users. Every evening, the barracks elder distributed the daily food rations, a kilo loaf of bread for four (later six, still later eight) people and a rancid square of margarine to feed twelve. Those who were able to restrain themselves saved half a slice of bread for the morning, so they could have it with the liter of tepid black water, called coffee, that they received for breakfast.

When my mother wanted to meet the girl I was courting, she invited us to her hut. It was a festive occasion, in spite of the noise made by the few hundred women who surrounded us. We sat on Mother's pallet and talked about the present, the past, and the days to come, as we savored an omelet with boiled potatoes. Mother wanted to commemorate the occasion even more. She left for a few minutes and returned with a pot of coffee.

"Mom, where did you get this 'dessert'?" I asked, after tasting the foul liquid. "It's real poison; I'm going to investigate."

There was a line in the corner of the hut, where an enterprising man was selling the coffee from a pail and not from the usual breakfast pot. The legend on the pail, SANITARY DETAIL, told me what I wanted to know. In the daytime, the man used the pail to scrub the floors with the aid of a strong disinfectant; in the evening, he dispensed coffee from it at a bargain price; at night, the same man and the same pail had steady subscribers who used it as a mobile toilet, when unable to make it to the latrine. He charged a moderate fee for this convenience. Who knows if the brigand ever bothered to wash the pail?

One morning, I couldn't muster enough strength to rise from my bunk, even for the vital need of joining the line for coffee. My throat was swollen, and my head refused to leave the pillow. This made me unfit for work, and the elder procured a medical slip allowing me two days of rest. However, soon after the morning assembly, I thought I heard my name being called. This was confirmed when I felt a tug on my legs and saw an SS man, who started screaming at me: "Get up at once. You made a mistake in copying and you must correct it before the commandant catches it — he's on his way to the office."

I knew the consequences of being caught! In my excitement, I forgot about being sick and jumped to my feet completely cured. I had to run the half kilometer to the office, while feeling my head and throat for signs of pain. It seemed that my illness was only in my mind. Luckily, the error was a minor one, easily corrected.

As I started to perform my customary work, I suddenly remembered the pass allowing me two days' rest. My coworkers urged me to take advantage of this valuable bonus and wanted to know how I'd managed to fool the doctor. It seemed too good an opportunity to miss! Alas, this was not to be; as soon as I lay down on my pallet again, I was seized once more by the previous symptoms, and my disability kept me in bed for . . . exactly two days.

We have reached the street that separates the men's and the women's camps. The usual electrified barbed-wire fences are strung on both sides. Please note the side entrance to the women's camp and the gate to the *Ordnung Dienst* — the hut of the Jewish police, which lies within the women's compound.

Before stopping there, we'll turn to the right to visit some other important sites that were sanctified by the blood of our brethren. First is Kamp Quarantäne, two "quarantine" huts (18, 19) and a latrine (20), all enclosed by barbed wire. Kamp Quarantäne used to be the new Jewish cemetery of Krakow. After the destruction of the ghetto in the last "action," on March 13, 1943, the Germans brought here those who had hidden in their homes and failed to report for the transports. A large pit had been prepared beforehand, and in it they killed more than two thousand people. They forced the residents of the adjacent huts to cover the victims with a layer of earth.

By the time my group arrived, the massacre was nearly over. The remaining headstones around the pit were splattered with blood and fragments of brains. Human arms and legs were sticking out from the surface of the mass grave. I saw a woman's hand, still stirring, pointing an accusing finger that was slowly rising, as if to warn the killers that their hour of reckoning would surely come. Victims of other, smaller "actions" were subsequently added to this mass grave, until it could absorb no more. Then the Germans put an old ditch to use, left over from World War I, for further executions. To add to the sacrilege in Kamp Quarantäne, they ordered a latrine built over the buried bodies.

Farther on, in a section carved out of the hill and made level, are the bathhouse (49), clothing depot (48), and delousing station (50). An excavator was used to prepare the site for building. The dug-up soil, which was removed to the other side of the hill, contained remnants of bodies from the cemetery, along with shreds of the prayer shawls in which they had been buried. The bodies, too, were deported from their shelters, as if they didn't deserve to rest in peace. We named the excavator operator "The Dentist," because he used a hammer to knock out the gold teeth he found in the unearthed skulls. My father, of blessed memory, met his death here; he was murdered by an SS man named Gruen. Inmates coined a phrase: "He went under the excavator," meaning that he was killed by the Germans. Should an innocent ask what was meant by the phrase, he would be informed sarcastically, "Haven't you heard? He refused to eat the pudding."

In the end, they replaced the old bathhouse with a large, "modern" facility. While it had two hundred showers, we were allowed to use them sporadically and only at night. The reason was the shortage of water, due to the fact that the camp was located on high ground at a distance from the water works, and the pipes were too narrow to carry the required amount. After depositing our clothing at the delousing station and coating our bodies with washing soda, which burned the million sores caused by the fleas, lice, and bedbugs, we would find there wasn't enough water, let alone warm water. Generally, two people shared a single shower, and each tried to get the maximum number of drops, shouting, "Water, water!" But the water just wouldn't flow. There were whisperings that the Germans turned off the main water tap out of spite, or the Kapo in charge of the showers was doing it for fun. However, often that wasn't necessary — there simply was no water. The delousing station also didn't function properly. The heat just never rose to a reasonable temperature. Once, I forgot a candle in my uniform. I was worried it would melt and spoil my only garment, but the candle survived unharmed, and so did the lice.

Ladies and gentlemen, as you can see, the road that used to lead to Graves Hall is closed. The electrified fence surrounding the living quarters stands in the way, so we'll now return in the direction of the women's camp. On the left is the *Appellplatz*. In the distance, above Bergenstrasse, is a row of huts in front of a green hill. The silence is interrupted only by the chirping of birds and the noise of moving trains, their whistling locomotives echoing in the distance. Wait, no . . . it isn't the chirping of birds; it's the squeaking of wheelbarrows. On the path to the mustering grounds I can see a large line of striped shadows pushing the wheelbarrows, and each one of them contains a nude body, whose bloody head is bouncing over the squeaking wheel. The other sound, I've just noticed, wasn't a locomotive; it was the whistle of an SS man. All the Kapos are shouting, "Line up in threes, line up!"

Near the rock crusher stands a black car holding the commandant, dressed in a white cap and white sweater, which bodes no
good. In the deadly silence, which has descended like a black cloud,
are rows upon rows of shaven heads topping striped pajamas. . . .
"Hey, you there, you goddamn sonofabitch, can't you hear me? Do
you want to go under the excavator?" Suddenly, I realize the Kapo is
addressing *me*.

I beg your pardon. It's nothing; I just remembered something
from my past. We'll be moving on to the women's quarters now. It's
nice out today, very quiet. Only the birds are chirping, and the noise
of the trains and the whistles of the locomotives echo in the distance.

We'll first enter the station of the OD, the Jewish police (14),
located within the women's compound. The chief officer was
Chilowicz, and his deputy was Finkelstein. Both were killed, together with their families, a few months before the destruction of
the camp. The Jewish policemen wore uniforms and visored caps
with yellow bands. They spewed curses incessantly. Whips were
their personal weapons, and they never let go of them. With the
whips' help, they enforced obedience during their work, which consisted of driving their own people to the selections and "actions."
They assisted the SS men in rounding up prisoners and guarding
them during the lockups. In return, they received the privilege of
sleeping with their wives in special cells that could be closed from
the inside, a double portion of thicker soup, and a loaf of bread with
jam. Once, when I was delivering a map of the camp to Chilowicz,
his men brought in a prisoner dressed in regular clothes, with a
white shirt, a tie, and a pair of shoes fastened together by their laces.
The man had apparently attempted to escape. Chilowicz beat him,
kicked him in the belly, and shouted, "Take a good look at this madman." I studied the hapless victim from the side, and he seemed

perfectly normal to me. I looked at the striped costumes that the rest of us wore and wondered who the crazy ones were.

The huts in the women's camp (Z) were arranged like the men's; there were three tiers of bunks, a stove, and a pail of water for use in case of fire. However, behind the stern appearance, behind the killings, hunger, and fear, there was a difference — an aura of romance. Sex was not in open evidence, as it was not of utmost concern, but nature followed its course and love existed, albeit clandestinely. At a time when death lurked in every corner, when fear made the heart tremble, there was no place for sentimentality. When the SS caught a couple making love, even in the early stages, when they sat holding hands or stood together in a dark corner, the punishment was a double execution. If a man was discovered in the women's camp after the gate had closed, he was killed at once; and there's no need to guess what awaited a pregnant woman. Pharaoh ordered the killing only of male offspring, but Hitler went much further. He forbade Jewish women to conceive, and destroyed the fetus together with the mother. All the same, roses grew in this minefield.

While working in the construction office, I stood outside one day, trying to make some sun prints. I aimed a large frame with a drawing backed by light-sensitive paper at the cloudy sky, waiting, in vain, for the sun to emerge. I was very tense. I never desired the sun more than on that day, for I would be at a loss to find a way to explain my failure to the Nazi supervisor, a known expert in murder, though not too skilled a builder.

At that fateful moment, a pretty girl, whose striped uniform didn't diminish her attractiveness, came out of the office, stopped before the frame that so yearned for ultraviolet rays, and asked, "What are you trying to do?" I replied, "I'm waiting for the reluctant sun to come out. Could you, perhaps, take its place?" Her reply was to flee in embarrassment.

This was my first meeting with my future wife, Rebecca, my

life's sunshine. The next morning, I gathered a bouquet of wildflowers, which I smuggled inside in my cap, and went to call on her. As a pretext, I planned to thank her for her help and let her know I had succeeded in making the copies after all.

However, before I could open my mouth, one of the clerks in the office grabbed the flowers from my hands and squashed them, then threw them into the waste can. "Get out of here, you nut! Don't you know that the commandant is in the next room?" With these words, he shoved me outside.

A few days afterward, I met my sun stand-in while waiting in line for soup. Later I kissed her for the first time, in full moonlight, behind the latrine. I began to call at her hut every morning before roll call. I brought her warm water from the kitchen and shined her shoes with my sleeve, dampened with spittle.

In the camp, there was this gender difference in dress: the male prisoners hid their baldness under a striped cap, while the females used a white kerchief to cover their shaven heads. I wore a cap but in my pocket always carried a white kerchief, my pass to the women's quarters. Our courtship lasted through actions and selections, during which we barely avoided a permanent parting several times. It took a series of miracles for both of us to survive.

I traded four loaves of bread for a silver spoon, and for four more, the jeweler in the watchmakers' shop fashioned two rings from it. That evening, we performed a mini-wedding by the side of my mother's bunk. There was no rabbi, no guests or music, no mayonnaise salad. I just pronounced the traditional "Harei At . . . ," and Mother gave us her blessing. Then I took my bride to her hut (13) to consummate our marriage. We climbed up to her pallet on the third tier and waited impatiently for lights out. To our chagrin, the barracks elder didn't put out the lights the entire evening — the Germans were combing the women's quarters for concealed men.

Strategic reasons made me conclude that it was too late to

attempt an escape, and no alibi could save me. We decided to cope with the situation by using a ruse. My wife's two neighbors covered me with all sorts of rags that usually served them as pillows, and I lay beneath their heads while the three of them pretended to be asleep. Of course, they got no sleep at all, for they were filled with terror, and their pillow kept quaking with fear under their heads. When the search was over, we heard the screams of two boys, who were beaten to death on the altar of Eros.

A miracle had saved me from being discovered. Then, when I tried to turn around in the bunk, we heard the siren calling the men to the mustering grounds. I jumped down from the top pallet in a single leap and, as I dashed out, covered my head with the white kerchief, so I could pass the guards without my identity being questioned. However, the electrified gate was shut! I stood there out of breath, out of ideas, out of hope. I knew only one thing for sure: If I didn't report to the assembly within a few minutes, this would be my last night on earth. If I attempted to scale the gate, the result would be the same, but my death would be swifter and more dignified.

As a floodlight beam swept past me, I made my decision. I said a hurried farewell to this cruel world, to my life, which had not really begun, and to my mother, my brother, and my bride, who would in a minute become a widow. Then I made my fateful leap. Fear made me soar over the humming fence. I rose, unwittingly, so high that only my fingers and toes grazed the strands with the lethal current. Before I landed on the other side, one of my trouser legs got caught on an upper barb and ripped apart; other barbs bit into the muscles of my skinny leg.

Another round of the floodlight ignored me as I lay prone on the ground. There was still the electrified barrier of coiled barbed wire, a meter in height, to conquer.

To this day, I cannot understand how I managed to cheat that mad trap, the dragon that spit fire and swallowed even the bravest heroes. By rights, I should have found my death then and there! When I reached the parade grounds, the loudspeakers announced that the *Appell* had been canceled.

Ladies and gentlemen, we are leaving the women's camp through its main gate (205), the same gate that was so cruelly closed on my wedding night. The steps you're descending are made of marble from broken Jewish headstones. The remnants of names on them want to tell you that the owners' skulls, deprived of their gold teeth, are seeking eternal rest under the laundry hut, together with bullet-ridden bones that never knew any monuments at all.

The laundry (23) served to wash the pants and shirts of the murder victims. Before sending them to the clothes depot, workers cleaned them of blood and sweat spots, replaced buttons that had fallen off when the wearers undressed under pressure, and patched the holes made by bullets. The Germans were fussy about order and neatness.

As for us, we had nothing to launder, because we wore the same striped clothes day and night; we couldn't part with them for laundering. This assured the bugs of ideal living conditions, of which they took full advantage, biting us without restraint or limit. They defied our vengeance, whether in the form of scratching our shaved skulls, rubbing our armpits, or scraping at our bodies, all done openly in the company of others. Hunting for bugs in the folds of our clothing was the only mass entertainment permitted at night by the authorities.

The laundry had a special department serving the SS teams and the important officers. Once, when the commandant sent his white sweater to be washed, the whole crew sat up through the night, watching it dry, so it wouldn't be stolen or fall to the ground or be prey to the devil knows what other mishap, before its delivery.

We are now at the commercial and cultural center of the camp: the latrine (27, 32), consisting of two huts, each thirty meters long. Within, on each side, were rough boards with thirty holes, without any partitions. The center was occupied by a trough, over which was suspended a pipe equipped with a series of spigots. Water was not always available, but every morning before roll call and every night after work you could meet most of the camp's inmates here.

At least two people used every tap, and a few others waited for them to finish. Sixty people sat over the holes and exchanged old news and new jokes, while making the noises that accompany bodily functions. They were surrounded by lines of the impatient, anxious to take their places.

Many important matters were settled in this latrine. Deals were made to exchange bread for cigarettes or sugar. If one was lucky enough to have some money, it was even possible to buy a hard-boiled egg, butter, or sticky candies produced mysteriously in some home factory. At times, in order to evict idlers, the Jewish cops, wielding whips, or SS men with drawn guns would barge in and create a general panic. Some people ran out half naked and wet, trying to dry their faces with their fingers. Others moved aimlessly, holding up their pants while their diarrhea kept flowing. "Dealers" chased after those who hadn't had time to pay for their purchases.

One winter day, the latrine was closed temporarily, and a long line of people needing to use it waited outside. Suddenly, the clouds parted and a few rays of sun spilled over the camp. A man in the line closed his eyes and lifted his face upward. This annoyed the SS man who happened to be passing by. He slapped the sun-worshiper in the face a few times and reprimanded him: "Haven't you learned yet the sun wasn't created for Jews?"

The cottage next to the latrine is the bakery (38). Once a community center for the Jewish children of Krakow, it was the first home of the Nazi commandant before he moved to the Red Villa.

After his departure, the engineer Greenberg was ordered to build two ovens, with a daily capacity of 4,500 loaves of bread. When the surviving Jews from the nearby ghettos were transferred to Plaszow, the increase of hungry inmates necessitated a third oven. Together the three ovens produced 6,000 loaves a day, to feed 24,000 inmates — a ration of 250 grams per person per day. The bread was a sort of dried dough formed from a mixture of brown flour and sawdust. To our hungry palates, this dark concoction assumed the flavor of a delicious cake.

Our world revolved around this ersatz bread; it became a medium of exchange on the black market near the latrine and the accepted currency for any purchase. It was also given to us as wages for our hard work. Once, the commandant, in an effort to speed up production, promised an increased portion of bread if we finished the project we were building in record time. In fact, we did get an increase, although not exactly the one he had promised: the number of people sharing a single one-kilo loaf was increased by two. Later, another twosome was added, which meant that eight hungry stomachs had to be satisfied with a single loaf!

At that time, an observer from the International Red Cross was touring the camp. When he asked the Jewish worker at the bakery how much bread each prisoner received daily, the commandant, who stood behind the observer, raised two fingers in order to help the baker supply the desired answer.

The bread distribution was so vital to our survival that it became a daily ritual, bordering on a religious service, conducted by each group of eight partners. One did the slicing, using a piece of sharpened metal, and the rest followed his every move, offering all sorts of advice on making a just division of the hallowed loaf. At times, the process was interrupted by arguments and fisticuffs, which required the intervention of the hut elder. Had the loaf been round, the cutting into eight equal pieces wouldn't have posed such

a problem, but it was oval in shape, and it called for another, more sophisticated procedure.

Each octet had a scale made of two tin cans attached by strings to a horizontal bar with a nail in the middle, which had to be held up by hand. No weights were used, so we never knew exactly how much bread we consumed in order to maintain our token existence. The baker claimed that each loaf weighed a full kilo, but we knew it was much less — after all, where else could he get the flour he set aside for the black market? In any case, this is how the cutting was done: First, the cutter made two halves, which were placed on each side of the scale. Then he added a crumb here and there to make them balance. When everyone approved, he kept slicing and weighing until the equal portions were ready to enter eight hungry mouths.

But that wasn't the end. Since there was always a suspicion that the pieces weren't one hundred percent equal, perhaps on account of the scale playing tricks, a lottery was held to award each his lucky share. One of the octet, already licking his chops in anticipation of the feast, was asked to turn around, and the game of chance began. The cutter pointed to one of the pieces at random and asked in Yiddish, *"Wehmen dus?"* — "Whose is this?" — and the one who had his back to us answered, also at random, "It's for him," and he pointed to one of the group, who eagerly caught the piece of bread tossed to him. The chanted query was repeated seven times, until only one piece was left for the cutter himself. The game would have been funny, had it not been so tragic.

Next to the bakery is the kitchen (37). This was the most important facility of the camp, and its employees were the most esteemed. Whatever his job, a kitchen worker was highly sought after as a friend or even a distant acquaintance. He might have been a floor sweeper, a potato peeler, or a dishwasher, but his status remained exalted. One who knew a kitchen worker became ipso facto a persona grata. Because our very life depended on it, *protekzia* in the kitchen was of utmost value. One who lacked it was unfortunate indeed.

I happened to be among the latter, so I had to make do with

the legal rations: a ladleful of tepid black water for breakfast, and for supper a liter of watery soup with some groats at the bottom, the color variable, depending on the kind of salt used. In the winter, the cooks used the greenish salt employed to melt the snow on the road; in the summer, the bluish kind served to cattle. The few groats that swam around in the liquid paid little attention to its hue. At times, there were changes in our diet. Now and then the Germans gave us "sago," small pills as transparent as mucus, without color, smell, or taste, but in appearance resembling frog eggs. For dessert, sometimes we had "jam," sour pink seeds, a by-product from the raspberry juice factory. When the herring factory supplied skins and entrails, our food was called "fish"; if some horses died in the stables, we had meat soup; when we spied barrels of spoiled sauerkraut that stank to high heaven, we knew we'd be eating cabbage soup for weeks. That particular odor was so disgusting that the smell of even the tastiest cabbage soup nauseated me for many years after the war.

When the Germans were expecting a visit from the International Red Cross once, they opened the food stores and for a limited time fed us the kind of rations to which we were entitled. The starved inmates blinked in disbelief at the sight of so much food and began gorging themselves on yellow cheeses, orange marmalade, cans of condensed milk, fresh eggs, and white sugar. Not being used to absorbing so many calories at once, they developed diarrhea. However, when the inspection was over, all this ended, never to return. We were treated again to the usual obnoxious diet, deficient in nutrition, taste, and color.

One day, walking past the kitchen, I noticed a commotion of excited people running in and out. I was told, in confidence, that a tank full of soup had spilled on the floor and was there for the taking. Unfortunately, I had no bowl with me, so I ran out to look for something suitable. All I found was a discarded chamber pot crowning a pile of junk outside the hospital. It was old and dented, and the handle was gone, but I cleaned it with sand and snow, wiped it with my sleeve, and attached a strip of cloth to hold it. Despite the time it took to do all this, I still managed to scrape up some remains of the precious delicacy from the floor.

Speaking of food, when later I was at the Brinnlitz camp in Czechoslovakia, we prisoners were turned into "Muslims" — so named in reference to the living skeletons we'd seen in newsreels of famine-ridden Muslim countries before the war — as the result of a diet devoid of vitamins, fats, and calories. Our bones wore nothing but a covering of skin infested with lice, fleas, and bedbugs. My weight went down to thirty-four kilos (seventy-five pounds). How did I know? Well, at the entrance to the showers and the delousing facility, the Germans placed a scale used for weighing sacks of food, barrels of liquid, or crates of other merchandise. Once a month, when we came to wash and to try ridding ourselves of the vermin, a Jewish cop ordered each of us onto the scale in order to detect the sly ones who had managed to scrounge food above the allotment. However, those who could manage this also managed to bribe the policeman with cigarettes, a roasted potato, or a dried beet. In exchange, he recorded a few kilos less when entering their weight. At one of the morning musters, the son of the camp commandant, Untersturmführer Joseph Liepold, denounced us in these words: "You're all robbers and thieves, every one of you. By rights, you should have been dead two months ago, but you keep on living. It's obvious you're gorging on food that belongs to the Germans, and someday we're going to catch you at it, you filthy rats!"

One night, my neighbor returned to his bunk from work and, instead of a greeting, yelled at me, "Hey, move over, you corpse." Then he sat down and withdrew from his pocket, with pride and satisfaction, a piece of meat lodged between two slices of white bread. He proceeded to eat this sandwich noisily, with annoying relish, ending with a burp and a prolonged fart. Suddenly, a man from an adjoining bunk sniffed the air and called out excitedly, "I smell the smell of a human being! This is the smell of a human being!"

The situation went from bad to worse. The number of groats in the soup diminished, and each day it looked less and less like soup. In the end, it tasted like warmed-over dishwater; even the colored salt was gone, and so was the smelly cabbage. Now some of the "Muslims" grew bloated and moved with difficulty, appearing either to be drawn to the muddy earth or to float upward into the filthy air of the camp. All arguments revolved around food; people tortured themselves and sharpened their unsatisfied appetites with memories of tempting delicacies replete with fat, sugar, and cream, consumed by them in days gone by. The norms of human conduct were forgotten, and the image of man was far away. In spite of this, we persisted, with a superhuman effort, to hope for the end of the war.

In the course of half a year, we destroyed the annex of the famous Hoffman Brothers' Czechoslovak cloth factory and replaced its modern machinery with giant equipment for producing antitank shell casings. However, in spite of the prompting and prodding of the foremen, not a single crate of our products reached the front lines. The managers of the factory, who had been appointed by the shrinking Greater Germany, were Oskar Schindler and his wife, the legendary couple who saved eleven hundred men and women, including us, from the claws of Goeth and the ovens of Gröss-Rosen. The Schindlers cared for us in a manner that surpassed our understanding, for it was beyond the comprehension of slaves who had forgotten their ever being free citizens. The Schindlers were an extreme rarity in the Nazi empire. They fed us at their own expense, but there was an end to this, too. We had already eaten all the horses that had succumbed to the area's great hunger, we had finished all the dried beet peels that had been intended for these horses (may their memory be blessed), and the time came when not a crumb was left to sustain life. Even the machines stopped working because they hadn't received their due — no materials, no spare parts. In short, the Final Solution was already knocking at our gates. When Untersturmführer Liepold and his SS underlings quit torturing us, it seemed highly suspicious. There were even rare cases of less rabid SS men trying to befriend prisoners, which created a real panic among us. The rumor was that Liepold was waiting for an order from Berlin, now under siege by the Russians, but it was doubtful that such an order would ever come.

At night, we heard explosions from the front, which was getting closer. We watched German trucks speeding in the opposite direction, a good omen. Abandoned, we lay listlessly in our crowded bunks. Even my neighbor lay quietly by my side, without his annoying burps or a single fart. I watched the flies on the ceiling waiting to pounce on a fresh corpse.

I remembered a dream of long ago, which I had dreamed before in similarly dire situations. Whenever I imagined departing from my present incarnation on this cruel earth, it always came back, always bearing its special meaning. The setting was several years before this historic upheaval. I was learning to chant the "Haftarah," a passage I had to read at my bar mitzvah. The melamed, as Hebrew teachers were called, had tried very hard to instill in me a love of that exotic alphabet, but my mind just couldn't absorb the funny print that ran backward. Even the pages of the book, which he kissed at the start of each lesson, turned the wrong way.

"Rebbe," I asked in Polish, "why is the Jewish language standing on its head; why is everything topsy-turvy?" The rebbe opened the book with exaggerated reverence, pointed to one letter *lamed* among other *lameds* scattered over the page, and answered in Polish, "Look at this *lamed*, which stands in the middle of the Hebrew alphabet; it's the only one that rises above the other letters, as if aiming upward. *Lamed* in the holy language is in the imperative tense and means 'Learn,' and whoever learns, learns, and learns soars to the highest strata."

At the time, I didn't understand much of this sermon. I never believed, for instance, as I followed the teacher's look upward, that I would be able to soar like a bird. All I saw was the ceiling, not some upper stratum. However, something did stir in my brain, and the letters assumed a new shape for me: they gained a third dimension and stood up proudly. Gradually, I started to delve into the strange phrases; I copied the lettering, with the added vowels, writing words I couldn't understand and composing sentences from the unexplored resources of the language. Something meaningful was developing in my mind, like a switch activating a powerful generator to create high tension.

After a few more lessons, I was able to read words whose meaning I hadn't yet learned, and my curiosity kept growing. All day I was haunted by parts of the prayers, which for me were the magic whisperings of a sorcerer. I felt enchanted by the guttural tongue murmuring within my brain, awakening echoes of generations past and overpowering my thoughts.

One morning, while I was still half asleep and lost in a dream, my ears caught the voice of someone unseen. Not yet able to write the words I heard in the original script, I spelled them phonetically in Polish on the edge of a newspaper. I wrote: "tagija lebetel." When the melamed arrived, I showed him what I had written in my dream. "I don't understand it — is it in the language of our ancestors?"

The melamed glanced quickly upward, then placed his hand on my head and looked me in the eyes with profound respect. "This great dream of yours is proof of my prediction. The 'voice' obliges you — in fact, it tells you — that someday you will reach Beth-El ["the home of God," in Hebrew]." Then he repeated the prophecy in Polish. Since then, as promised from above, I have crossed safely all the rivers of Babylon, rivers filled with suffering and torture. I knew all the time that a place was reserved for me at some hallowed but remote destination.

Even on that particular day, when I felt that I had reached the end of my rope, I recalled in my inner ear the voice that had commanded a more generous fate for me. Will divinity disappoint me again? I wondered.

At the very last minute, my destiny remembered me; it grabbed me by the collar and literally yanked me out of the arms of death. With a desperate effort, I got up from my bunk and, supporting myself against the wall, went downstairs to the yard. I saw a group of Jews digging a deep pit and asked what was happening. "We don't know," they replied.

At that moment, Schindler, the director, came up to me and gave me a bottle of expensive wine wrapped in wicker. Nodding his head toward the office of Untersturmführer Liepold, he said, "Give him this bottle of urine." I got the message and followed his order. Only because Liepold got drunk and passed out, his frightened aides having deserted, did he fail to execute the final instructions from burning Berlin: "Finish off the Jews!"

The pit, which had already been lined with lime, remained empty, and we, the eleven hundred prisoners, were selected for life. Two days later, we opened the main gate for the first Russians, who brought us flowers atop their bayonets and offered us freedom. Thus ended the years of slaughter, and from that day on the sun shone for the Jews as well.

Ladies and gentlemen, we are now entering the infirmary (21,

22) of Plaszow. We gave it the lofty title of "hospital," which it certainly didn't deserve. The Germans kept the sick here in order to prevent epidemics, and in the event of an "action," they didn't have to go looking for the "idlers" in the barracks — the transport to the ovens was already assembled here. The Germans had no intention of maintaining hospitals, or even clinics, for the benefit of the inmates. In plain words, the infirmary served as a way station for those condemned to death. The doctors, under SS supervision, helped the sick to die sooner and without any interference. I must say in their favor that in those days, dying in bed was considered a luxury.

If anyone deluded himself that he would be cured here, his first contact with the installation made it obvious that, without medicines, without equipment, and without goodwill, no one could be helped. Generally, the doctors and nurses took care of wounds and bruises caused by beatings, as well as crushed bones and broken limbs. Not every victim of bloody injuries was sent here; at times, the commandant dispatched such a one to the quarries, for the wounds to jell during hard labor, or he administered a coup de grâce with a bullet to the head and a kick in the rear. The two huts off to the side (1, 4) were intended for infectious diseases. Only one cure was available — an injection of benzine or gasoline.

Visits to the infirmary were rare. Perhaps the skimpy diet helped protect us from ordinary illnesses. It could also be that the cruel treatment inured us to things we would have suffered from before the war — or made us more reluctant to acknowledge weakness. People were ashamed even to admit that their muscles stuck to their bones, that they were at the end of their mettle. To do so meant belonging to the category of "idlers," who refused to work and could be sentenced to death by hanging or butchery, without resort to the hospital.

Our garb consisted of striped uniforms made of thin unlined

fabric guaranteed to be free of cotton, a cap of the same material, and wooden clogs without laces or socks. Neither undershirts nor underpants were issued, and coats and sweaters were banned. If a person was discovered wearing anything under the striped garment, it was the last time he wore anything at all. His naked body was thrown into a pit, and the uniform was laundered and stored for future use. If a woman wore a bra or panties, the SS men painted her breasts red.

During the winter rainstorms we got soaked to the bone, and when it snowed we turned into blocks of ice. In spite of this, I don't recall ever having a cold or flu, a runny nose, or a coughing fit. It may be that I really did get sick, but other sufferings took precedence over these symptoms.

With the aid of *protekzia* and a loaf of bread, I once managed to be admitted to a dental clinic in order to secure a filling for an aching tooth. While I sat in the chair, the SS man in charge of the clinic looked in my mouth and ordered, "Extract a front tooth without anesthetic." This was done at once. I was afraid to object or cry out in pain during the extraction of that perfectly healthy tooth. After this episode, my affected tooth never hurt me again.

The empty lot behind the infirmary was intended for a crematorium (K). All the components had already arrived, but the knights of the superior race failed to complete this modern and efficient tool for the Final Solution.

We are now moving on to the Gorka Chujowa (206), "Prick Hill," a place sanctified by the deaths of thousands of Jews killed by the Nazis, whether by fire or sword, by wild beasts or hunger, thirst, epidemics, strangulation, or stoning. The vulgar nickname of this historic site derives from the name of the SS man Huyar, which sounded like *chuj*, or prick, in Polish. Perhaps by calling it this, the prisoners wanted to express their helplessness in the face of the degradation and cynicism of the world that ignored them.

The Germans used two dugouts left over from World War I here for mass graves in which countless people were driven to slaughter and immolated. The established procedure was as follows: The victims were brought to the dugouts in groups. Those from the first group undressed, handed over their clothes, put down a layer of logs, and lay side by side, to be shot with machine guns. The second group undressed, covered the dying with another layer of logs, and lay down the same way. So it went with one group after another, until the last one was forced to pour gasoline over the bodies and light a bonfire before their own deaths. No one uttered a cry, because the Germans had taken care to plug their mouths with plaster. Once, one of the condemned miraculously escaped and described how the *Wachmans* (Russian prisoners who cooperated with the Nazis), after killing seventy Jews from the town of Bonarka, stood in line for the pleasure of raping a dead Jewess. "Faster, faster," they urged, "while she's still warm."

From this elevation, the whole camp can be seen. You can gaze beyond the barbed-wire fence at the houses and streets of free Plaszow. In the days of Commandant Goeth, we never stopped to look at a landscape; we were Hitler's slaves doing slave labor in all the cruel meaning of the term, and in our degradation, we were prohibited from enjoying a moment's rest. When any foreman or underling ordered someone to cross a street, it was done on the run. On meeting a bearer of the Nazi symbol, a Jew had to remove his cap, stand at attention, and call out his number, the nature of his work, and his destination. Under the best circumstances, such a meeting ended with a kick in the behind or a brutal slap in the face. Another thing to prevent us from surveying the scenery was the daily bonfires on the Gorka Chujowa, which filled the air with the stench of burning flesh and clouds of choking smoke.

Today the camp is quiet. No more hammering, no shooting,

and no German curses; this industrial area is wrapped in silence. But in those days, when the oiled wheels of the murder apparatus ground up tens of thousands of Jews, who had first been deprived of their property, in totally useless slaughter, there lived a wise Jew by the name of Yitzhak (Isaac) Stern, who, with the help of Mietek Pemper and the engineer Sigmund Greenberg, suggested to Commandant Goeth that the camp could play a constructive part in the conduct of the war. Instead of killing Jews, the Germans could use them and their machinery, which was still stored in the ghetto, to manufacture ammunition. The idea didn't help the German war effort much, but it saved the lives of some twenty thousand Jews who were destined for murder.

In order to prepare plans for the shops that would be needed, we in the construction office labored nonstop for several days and nights. The authorities accepted the plans and ordered materials sufficient to make the workshops that were then erected. Here, in the first row, close to Bergenstrasse, are the locksmith and tinsmith shops (84). Next to them are the foundry (89), the central storage depot (85), the shoe factory (82), the watchmakers' (83), and the electricians' (87). On the opposite side are the carpenter sheds (91, 94), the printing shop (92), and the brush factory (95). This industrial complex was subsequently expanded by seventeen huts for tailors, furriers, and upholsterers.

Several months later, there was a new development. The work camp, where murder was already rampant, became an official concentration camp, replete with ingenious installations for destroying human beings. We were transferred from the authority of the regional constabulary to the hands of the German police and the SS, those experts in mass extermination. The place received the official title of Plaszow Concentration Camp, and we were issued the striped uniforms of regular prisoners. The commandant was awarded permanent status, which exempted him from frontline duty. The workshops also received official sanction, so it was no longer necessary to conceal their role in the war effort.

From then on, our shops carried out maintenance work in the camp as well as filling private orders of SS personnel and the highest-ranking officers. The tailors produced made-to-measure uniforms, while the cobblers made and repaired shoes for the commandant, his friends, and subordinates. The printers published under-

Monument erected at the site of the Plaszow concentration camp. The legend neglected to mention that the prisoners were mainly Jews.

ground literature, presumably for the provocateurs, death sentence notices, and all sorts of classified forms. The central storehouse contained neatly arranged items of stolen Jewish property — cameras, watches, gold teeth, kitchen utensils, etc. It also housed the possessions of former humans who had yet to go "under the excavator" or up to the Gorka Chujowa.

Because of this storehouse and other caches, Commander Goeth was later confined to a German jail on the charge of thievery. According to a Jewish adage, he should have been acquitted, because stealing from a thief is no crime. However, the German high court thought otherwise — it held that the plundered Jewish property belonged to the state. By the end of the war, Goeth had landed in a Polish jail, and he was hanged after a brief trial.

We are now returning to SS Strasse. Up ahead, on the left, stand the villas of the officers who aided Goeth in his career. In the Red Villa, his home, Goeth filled crates with Jewish treasures for himself. Behind the Red Villa were kennels for the dogs (180) trained to attack people dressed in stripes, which were fed a daily diet of meat and noodle soup. When a Jew had to say something about a dog to a German, he had to preface the beast's name with "Mister," while he himself was just a number. He might say, "Mister Rolf is bored in his kennel today."

The buildings off to the right are stables (138), garages (132), chemical labs (130, 131), book storehouses (133, 134), pigsties (137), and enclosures for geese (140) and rabbits (139). We are again passing the Gray House, which is located between the barracks and the ruins of the funeral home. Now we're approaching the main gate and the road leading to the free world, to our present reality, so each one of us can return to his or her private life.

That's it, ladies and gentlemen; you have toured the entire camp. But this was just scratching the surface, one tear from a sea of tears. To describe the Plaszow camp correctly is a task equal to single-handedly raising a skyscraper, a building filled with the suffering of thousands of Jews.

Good-bye! You are leaving "My Plaszow," as it is engraved in my mind and stored in my memory, as I keep living it over and over again in my constant nightmares.

THE PARTING

Though our life together was so short,
I must leave now.
Sad and forlorn, I am going
to a fate ordained by these desperate times,
by a road unmarked by any signs,
to a mocking destiny
all set to welcome me.

I am going, but when the gate closes behind me
and a momentary silence reigns,
when time erodes my footprints,
don't think of me with sorrow
because I leave behind so little of myself:
the heart of a mad poet,
a few letters, a few odes dedicated to you,
a withered flower and the dreams we dreamt
of our future together,
and plans that alas! could not come true.
Do you remember our dream house
that was not to be,
your workroom and my workroom?
Dear God, why can't you be kind?

But if things change, as I foretold,
and if the memory lives on in your mind,
think of me often,
without the despair that is our lot now.

Our roads will yet meet again.
Then . . . but why are you crying?
Cry no more, don't be sad. . . .
Because, you see, I'm holding back too. . . .
Well, good-bye, I will see you again!
Give me another kiss and a hug
and take care of yourself,
my dear and sacred love.

NOTE: The author wrote this poem for his wife when they were to be separated on the shutting down of the Plaszow concentration camp.

It was Rebecca Bau who found a place for her husband on Schindler's list. When Amon Goeth heard that Rebecca could do manicures, he summoned her to give him one. He placed a gun at her elbow and told her that if she nicked or scratched him, he would shoot her on the spot. Though she was afraid and sometimes hid, she became his manicurist. Through this job, she came to know members of the house staff, among them Goeth's Jewish secretary, Mietek Pemper. One day Rebecca saw a Nazi guard about to shoot Pemper's mother. She intervened, warning the guard that if Goeth found out who he had killed, he would execute *him*. Pemper's mother told her son, and when the list of Jews that Oskar Schindler would be allowed to take with him to his factory in Czechoslovakia was being drawn up, Rebecca went to Pemper and reminded him of the favor he owed her. He agreed; but when he went to put down her name, she substituted her husband's instead. Many years later, after the release of the film *Schindler's List,* she told a journalist that she had had faith in her own survival, but she feared for her husband: "My husband was more important to me than I was, and I wasn't afraid." That was the first time Joseph Bau learned how he came to be spared the ordeal of the Gross-Rosen concentration camp.

Rebecca Bau was sent to Auschwitz, where she was marked three times for the gas chamber but talked her way out of certain death. During a selection, Josef Mengele took a red spot on her breast to be a sign of illness and pointed her to the line of those to be gassed. She went in the direction of the line, but circled back to the group of naked women still to be examined. Thrice she presented herself and was selected for death. The last time Mengele recognized her and became furious, but she wasn't afraid. She told him she wasn't sick, that the pimple was because she was menstruating. Dubious, because he said women in the camps stopped having periods, Mengele had a Polish woman perform a test with a rag. When the Polish woman verified her story, the "Angel of Death" relented and let Rebecca Bau go to the line of the living.

A FATEFUL REUNION

Thanks to Oskar Schindler, the savior of Jews, and to the heroic Russian army, the sealed gates of the Brinnlitz concentration camp, where I was interned, burst open for all eternity. We, the liberated inmates, still wearing our striped uniforms, dispersed in all directions, but not before emptying the stores of Jewish property looted by the German soldiers. I joined a trio of comrades, and each of us lugged suitcases filled with possessions that became ours when the world of their provisional keepers fell apart. We had no particular goal, and we didn't know the geography where fate had cast us.

Suddenly, on the horizon, we spotted a freight train moving through the unfamiliar landscape. Ignoring the fact that, because of prolonged hunger and dehydration, I scarcely weighed thirty kilos (sixty-six pounds), I started to run with my load, which must have weighed at least twice as much as me. I had made the spontaneous decision to head for my native city of Krakow, where I hoped to find my family waiting for me impatiently, and I was anxious to get on the train. I ran across plowed fields, pushed my way through bushes, and jumped over fences and railroad ties, until, in a state of utter exhaustion, I reached the last car. With my final measure of strength, I heaved my burden and myself aboard, just as the train decided to take a short break and stopped. When the engine began to pull again, I discovered that the car I was in had been uncoupled. I was left behind. When my companions caught up with me, they couldn't stop marveling at how I'd managed to get so far ahead of them, while they all but lacked the energy to follow.

Later that night, another freight train came by. Without asking the crew where it was headed, we pushed our way into a car already crowded wall to wall with passengers and baggage. In total darkness, while shaking with the movement of the train, we tried to learn from the people nearest us where we might find ourselves in the morning, but the answers only added to our confusion. However, from somewhere in the dense crowd a voice boomed out, providing the information we sought. The man who spoke was apparently a smuggler, who knew the district well. He advised us to get off with him at the station after the next, Morawska Ostrowa. From there, we could walk to the Polish-Czech border. It turned out to be good advice, as we soon reached a barbed-wire fence manned by guards. They scrutinized us and our papers, as well as every item of our luggage. Following the inspection, we were allowed to repack the suitcases and cross the border. Hurray! We were finally home! The signs spoke to us in Polish, and we no longer needed clumsy interpreters.

Our "guide" vanished from sight, but he couldn't be of help to us anymore. The locals treated us with friendship and understanding after learning we were Holocaust survivors. A few more miracles had to occur before we reached Krakow, but when we arrived, we

parted company hurriedly, without embraces or hugs, and each of us headed for what used to be his home.

Full of excitement, I ran toward the street where I was born, to the house where I grew up. Nothing had changed, but our former neighbors, whom I met in the corridor, whispered to me that our apartment was now occupied by the caretaker, who kept a knife handy by the door. He had moved in right after my father handed him the key, when the German conquerors forced us to move to the ghetto. I asked no more questions. The neighbors seemed glad to see me alive and offered to put me up until the rest of the family arrived. They also gave me the address of the Jewish Committee, where I could inquire about the fate of my relatives. It took a few visits there and scanning all the lists of survivors before I found out that my mother had died at Bergen-Belsen after the liberation. The American soldiers felt sorry for the emaciated inmates and fed them copious amounts of rich foods. However, their shrunken stomachs weren't able to digest the delicacies, and in one day ten thousand died from overeating. My brother Marcel was somewhere in Germany, and my wife, Rebecca, had left Lichtwerden, the Czech concentration camp, and was injured when the wagon she was in turned over. She was now in a hospital in Freudenthal.

Without taking time to change from my striped camp uniform, I secured a permit to go to Czechoslovakia and set out in search of my wife. Traveling by freight train, the accepted method in those days, I again found myself in Morawska Ostrowa. In a mixture of Polish and Czech, I asked the stationmaster how to get to Freudenthal. The red-capped official pointed to a train that was just leaving and said, "Take this train to Szwinow. There you must jump off while it's still moving and transfer to a passenger train to Freudenthal."

I sat down in the open doorway of a car, my feet dangling outside. Overcome by fatigue, I fell asleep in this dangerous position. When I woke, I realized that I must have passed the place where I was to have jumped off. It also turned out that the other train was under way on the opposite track, so I would have missed it in any case. I got off at the next station and asked a group of workers how to get to Szwinow. In reply, they burst out laughing and told me that it was far away, but they pointed to a train that was just starting off in the direction I had come from. This time, in order not to miss my stop again, I picked a flatcar without a roof. This turned out to be a poor choice, as it started pouring rain and hail; I was drenched to the core when I arrived in Szwinow and boarded a passenger train. I chose a window seat and, being exhausted and hungry, promptly fell asleep again. Thus I was still in my seat when the conductor ordered everyone off the train. From his explanation in Czech, I gathered that the train I had missed was crossing a bridge when it collapsed, plunging the train into the river. No one knew yet how many passengers had drowned and if there were any survivors. As for us, a bus would take us in the morning to the other side of the river.

Suddenly, a woman seeing my striped uniform accused me of being a German who had escaped from a camp where those accused of war crimes were being held. My protestations that I was a Jewish survivor of a concentration camp were to no avail. She kept shouting abuse and dragged me to the police station. The duty officer examined my papers and, satisfied I was telling the truth, asked how he could be of help. I told him my story about the search for my wife, who had been injured in an overturned wagon.

"You know," he said, "here in Opawa we had a similar accident with a wagon. In fact, there are still several girls in the hospital." I asked if they might know my wife; possibly they came from the same camp. In answer, he ordered a policeman to escort me to the hospital. Thus ended my search . . . for there I found Rebecca.

I've tried to describe our reunion, but words have failed me. How can one depict a miracle? I've scanned dozens of pages of recollections from that happy day. I kept correcting sentences and paragraphs and correcting the corrections, but nothing I could say sufficed. I tried to tell of the Czech woman who dragged me to the police station on account of my striped uniform and caused me to meet Rebecca in Opawa instead of going on to Freudenthal after the train that had plunged into the river without me; of how I entered the hospital with the policeman and whistled the tune we'd used to locate each other at the Plaszow camp. . . .

No, I cannot find the words to describe that wonderful reunion, which defied all the laws of nature. I'll leave it to you, dear reader, to imagine what happened on that fateful evening of June 7, 1945. . . .

"To my most precious wife on the day of our happy reunion after seven months of separation and six years of bondage."
This is the dedication I wrote in the book of poems presented to my wife at our reunion. The book was the size of a cigarette pack, and I had written it by hand in the Plaszow concentration camp.

THE GREAT HUNGER

My multipleated trousers bound to my bony hips by a shoelace,
hiding the shape of my old belly,
like a petrified lump of bread in a ragged pocket.

Hunger has built its nest in my desolate entrails.
It has become fruitful and multiplied,
filling my insides with
thousands of burning hungers.

Hey! Unplug my mouth!
I'm going to gulp down all the granaries in the world.
Breakfast . . . lunch . . . dinner . . .
I'll join the everlasting royal banquet.
I'll gorge myself without restraint,
use my nails for forks to grab the browned, fat meats,
spiced with dill and garlic,
the hot peppered sauces, giving off their tingly, heavenly odors,
the creamy cakes covered with melted butter . . .
and more cakes to tickle my palate,
fried onion sauces with mayonnaise salads and meats,
roasted, cooked, fried, and smoked.

Here come the appetizer, the entrée, and more,
millions of meals, meat and dairy:
May my ears shake with gluttony
and my thirsty eyes fill with lust.
May my chin drip with thick, gluey fat

I'll wipe with neither hand nor sleeve.
May the craving of my tongue fill city squares,
with or without a "bon appétit!"
Eeerup! I'll let out a mighty burp and cry,
"Ladies and gentlemen, just a bit more, until I'm sated."

Meanwhile, I luxuriate in meals digested long ago.
With hands raised to heaven,
I beg for alms like all the world's beggars,
who would bring forth bread from the earth,
though by devious means.

Dear God, have you ever gone hungry?

THE WORLD KEPT ITS SILENCE

"I never realized there are so many lame people in our city," said an acquaintance who was obliged to use crutches for a time. For while his legs were healthy and functioned perfectly, he failed to see the unfortunate ones, the lame and the hobbling. Only when he himself was afflicted did he become aware of their misery.

Some years before the war, owing to a dictatorial regime, there were many prisoners in our country's jails. My father once took me for a walk in order to work up an appetite before dinner. We happened to pass by a prison whose windows were enclosed with iron bars.

"The people who sit in there have nothing to lose," my father said. "Let's cross the street and avoid the danger of getting hurt."

I obeyed without asking what he meant by "the people who sit in there have nothing to lose." I didn't understand, though — if they didn't sit there, would they have something to lose? I tried to analyze the wisdom hidden in his words, but without success.

The expression bothered me for several years, at a time when I was just beginning to get a first taste of life, before I had made official acquaintance with the world. Only when the Germans put me behind their bars did I grasp what Father meant by his warning, though I didn't agree with him. When I found myself within the enclosure, many problems hitherto insoluble to me became clear. Dressed in prison garb, I viewed the world in a different light, but the world also regarded me with different eyes.

Once, after the evening roll call in the camp, at the end of one of the many sorrowful days we experienced, I stood with my wife at the gate to the women's barracks.

"Look — the world is keeping its silence. They're killing us here without shame, and the world is keeping quiet." After uttering this, my wife looked to me for an answer to her grave accusation. Her pained expression pierced my thin layer of hope, as if only on account of me were the people who shared my fate suffering, as if my striped appearance played a crucial part in this shameful drama.

"Well, what have you got to say?" she insisted, with raised chin and pursed lower lip. I tried to avoid the meeting of our eyes. I knew I couldn't come up with a suitable answer, knew that all the good tidings I'd been feeding her in wholesale quantities in order to encourage and fortify her would go down in defeat in their duel with reality. All the fresh news from the underground radio, which promised a second front and an end to the war, would collapse like the Maginot Line. I had no answer, but I refused to wave a flag signaling the defeat of my beliefs.

The answer from international Information . . .

My position was that of a merchant who has sold his customer a defective product and, instead of clearing his conscience by confessing that he has himself been fooled by the false advertising, keeps praising the product and its many uses, without admitting that it's coming apart between his fingers and the pieces are falling on the counter.

By this time we were used to the tortures, and death was a familiar guest in our houses. We were resigned to our bitter fate, which had been decided by an international lottery and had caused us numberless losses, shame, and public ridicule. We no longer expected that some miraculous power, some messiah, would appear to lead us out of there. We had started to believe that there must be a reason for our receiving the meanest portion when destinies were distributed. Every sort of transfer to the upper world became understandable and acceptable. For instance, in the case of Moshe the carpenter, the SS man split his head with a hammer because he didn't like the way Moshe had attached his personal number to the striped uniform. The redhead from the upholstery shop was hanged because they found a potato in his pocket. Really, why did Moshe sew his number on crooked — didn't he know the German passion for order and cleanliness? And how did the potato find its way into the redhead's pocket? It was certain he hadn't bought it in a grocery store or found it on the street. He must have stolen it, and if he stole, let that be a lesson to him. Lately we had stopped looking for reasons or asking why? Those who wanted to keep on living saw the light. "This is destiny," they said, "and there's no use resisting it. The Almighty decided, after careful consideration, to get rid of us and to issue a permit for the destruction of His people."

I made an impromptu decision to tell my wife why the world was keeping quiet and answered her with a query of my own: "Tell me: before the war, when you were a free person and your own mistress, what did you do for the victims of violence and oppression? I

remember, for instance, one Sabbath evening when we sat around the table, where candles flickered. We went through the entire ritual, and then an aromatic cake, filled with all sorts of sweets and iced with glittering sugar, appeared on the fine tablecloth. Mother, who was beaming with pride, began to cut her masterpiece, with the ceremony due a work of art. We emitted an 'ah' of pleasure as each received a fat slice. Father licked his lips in anticipation, opened his mouth, revealing shiny gold teeth, and took his first bite.

"Just then, the music on the radio was interrupted by the announcer, who reported, 'We have just learned that, by way of a miracle, an eyewitness, a victim of the Fascist regime just across the border, which is headed by a cruel tyrant, has escaped to tell his story. He has described the inhuman conditions and the atrocities inflicted on millions of innocent citizens and appealed to the free world to put a stop to the murders and sadistic tortures. People are foraging in the garbage for food, dead bodies are strewn all over, and there's no drinking water. . . . An epidemic is feared. . . . The indifferent international community is keeping its hands clean and ignoring this painful affair.'

"During the broadcast, Father kept the piece of cake in his mouth and looked at us with reproach, as if to say, 'And you think you're doing us a favor when you eat these delicacies? Do you hear what's going on over there?' His mouth full of cake, he met Mother's eyes. . . . A few creases appeared on his forehead, as he tuned his ears to hear more. But the radio resumed the gay dance music, and Father started to chew in time, like in a Charlie Chaplin movie. All of us continued eating the cake, with a loud smacking of lips, and we soon forgot the unpleasant interruption of our Sabbath meal. And it might have been that at that very moment, a young, hungry couple was looking around at the slain, blood-spattered bodies, and the woman was saying with despair, 'Well, as you can see, the world is keeping quiet.'"

My wife tightened the kerchief covering her shaven scalp, ran a fist over her creased forehead, and said with embarrassment, "Yes, in those days I didn't know, couldn't imagine, what it meant to destroy a people, but now I'm getting my comeuppance. Of course I care. Now I would know what to do."

Since that time I have discarded many calendars, our globe has made dozens of orbits around the sun, tons of multicolored inks have recorded the history that keeps moving forward, and states have ceased to exist while new ones have taken their places.

After that evening, hundreds of Saturday evenings have come and gone. A couple of nights ago, I sat around the table with my wife and children by the light of flickering candles. We went through the usual ritual, and a cake stuffed with sweets and iced with glittering sugar appeared on the fine tablecloth, and we greeted it with "ah"s. My wife beamed with pride as she started to cut the cake into fat slices with the ceremony due a work of art. I licked my lips with anticipation and opened my mouth to take the first bite.

Then the music on the radio was interrupted by an announcement: "We have just learned that, by way of a miracle, an eyewitness, a victim of the Fascist regime just across the border, which is headed by a cruel tyrant, has arrived to tell his story. He has described the inhuman conditions and atrocities inflicted on the innocent citizens and appealed to the conscience of the world to stop the sadistic tortures and murders. People are starving and foraging in the garbage for food, dead bodies are strewn all over, and there's no water. . . . An epidemic is feared."

I looked at my wife while the cake stuck in my mouth, and I saw her frightened, embarrassed expression. She shrugged her shoulders and gestured helplessly with her hands.

Suddenly, I saw her in the striped dress, with a white kerchief on her shaven head, looking at me with sad, hollow eyes. The light dimmed, and emaciated shadows dressed in prison uniforms surrounded me again. The chill wind brought the sound of shooting from the distance, and my nostrils breathed in the smell of burning flesh. I raised my hand to my chin, opened my mouth, and spit out on my fingers a few pieces of stone disguised as Sabbath cake.

The radio resumed its dance music, and the children savored the cake with loud smacking noises. But I dwelled for another long hour in the concentration camp that lies buried deep within my being.

THE INFIRMARY

Lying on their bunks, shriveled,
stained with shining perspiration,
withered dying bodies, too weak to groan,
in appearance no longer human:
Gone is their will to live, these deformed bodies,
once created in the image of God.
A plague devours what the lice haven't finished,
in the living skeletons on sale to death.

Expectation wears the Kapo's uniform.
Girded by an apron soaked with blood and pus,
he walks with heavy, monotonous steps
through the length and breadth of the hut,
counting the last minutes of the departing
and the places they will vacate.

One, two, three . . .
This one not yet, that one not yet . . .
Four, five, six —
maybe tomorrow for six . . .
This one by dawn . . .
Seven, eight.
That's all for now.
Eight numbers crossed from the list
and a comment noted:
"Died of their own free will."

On the nearby furnace,
fried souls are dancing
the hora of the mad vampires
with the black smoke,
fried souls that only yesterday
were discharged from the infirmary.

HAMSIN
A HEAT WAVE

The sky, hiding behind a cloud of sand, pretended to be indifferent toward events on the earth below. Since morning, a fan cut through the humid air and ground it into minuscule particles. Wide-open doors and windows extended a polite invitation to the draft, but the wind lay napping among the trees that had fainted on the avenue. A tired clock slowly ticked away the time, stretching the hours of business to their limit. Rivers of bottled soda water poured into the throats of clerks, who cooled their faces by fanning official forms. The heat dominated all conversations and arguments. Everyone agreed, as in past seasons, that even the oldest veterans couldn't recall a hamsin such as this.

At last, the sun, flushed with the effort, ended its day of torrid work and descended behind the horizon to take a rest. Night enveloped the city, but the hamsin kept up its onslaught, as if working overtime after the sun forgot to take it along. The streets filled with people, who inhaled the remnants of a breeze in every corner where it managed to evade the hamsin. The sidewalk cafés overflowed with customers, and the waiters wound their way skillfully with full trays among the gossiping ice cream swillers.

On such an evening, as was my custom, I made my way home after leaving the office. Just as I did every weekday, I stopped at the grocery to purchase the items on my wife's shopping list. The lazy grocer kept wiping his shiny forehead with an oil-stained apron and slowly arranged my purchases on the counter: a kilo of potatoes, white cheese, tea bags, a kilo of red apples (Do you have Jonathans? . . . No, no, we don't like Delicious), coffee (Not this; my wife likes decaffeinated instant), chocolate with nuts, bread (But only freshly baked kimmel with a soft crust. . . . Mister, why are you giving me dry bread left over from yesterday?), candles, cookies (The crisp ones, not too sweet and not too creamy; we're on a diet).

I watched as the storekeeper waited on me unhurriedly, with scant energy . . . and my attention drifted to the shelves, loaded with goodies in fancy packages, designed to lure the eyes of customers. Loud posters sought to entice me to buy more, even of things we didn't need. Every poster, like a professional barker, extolled the quality of the product it featured. All proclaimed with exaggerated certainty the virtues of what they were trying to sell, claiming it to be the best in the world, the cheapest, the healthiest, a thing of prestige. What is more, free gifts were offered: a car, a luxury apartment, a trip to America.

I kept looking, but I suddenly recalled a store of another kind — the grocery in the ghetto. That store was rich in confusion and poor in merchandise. The faded posters mourned quietly the delicacies that had disappeared from our menus long before. Such available items as saccharin, matches, washing soda, salt, and ersatz tea (a suspect liquid with an odd taste) needed no advertising.

Sometimes it was possible to obtain at this store, for a price, a kind of stony loaf we called "bread" in those times. One winter day, when a mighty frost joined forces with the Nazis, a rumor persisted that this bread would be sold at the grocery the next day. By 4 A.M., I'd become an integral part of a long line of hungry customers. Hundreds had come earlier and managed to occupy more advanced positions. Behind me the line kept growing along the sleep-cloaked lanes as people felt their way in the dark in search of its end. An icy wind penetrated the scarves and rags, to pinch the martyred faces. In order to cope with the bone-chilling cold, I had to stamp my feet in the freezing mud that covered the sidewalks. We were like solid mini-icebergs, as we hugged ourselves to keep warm. I inhaled the steamy breaths of the clinging shadows, on guard against anyone who might try to push ahead. All the same, at first light I spotted a new back intruding between me and the lame man who had stood in front of me. I was too tired to argue; the scarf that covered my ears, mouth, and nose had turned into a sheet of ice, and my toes had detached themselves from my authority.

At last, they opened the store, and the first ones in line burst inside. There were pitiful cries by people being crushed in the forward surge. Fists were raised. Some oldsters slipped and fell, only to be pushed aside by the throng. We started to advance at a snail's pace. The lucky ones clutched loaves of bread through their torn gloves. A sour smell perfumed the air, but to us it was tempting and mouthwatering. Our clogs made a scraping noise as we inched forward. I had already passed the arrogant sign DELICATESSEN AND PASTRIES. The lame man was inside, hugging a loaf to his chest, while the one who had taken my place was being served.

Just then, the storekeeper pierced the air with a cry: "That's it, there's no more!" To prove his point, he waved his empty basket in the air, indicating that no tears or pleas would help. In his overbearing way, he started to push us outside the store, toward the solid wall of disappointed customers still trying to press their way ahead.

"There's no more, can't you see? Go to hell, you creeps!" he yelled, mixing his curses with a spray of spittle flying in all directions. Then, instead of bread, he started to distribute liberal kicks and blows among the hungry, frozen humans.

"Is that all, sir?" I was brought back to reality by the voice of the Tel Aviv grocer, wiping his forehead with his greasy apron. "I'm tired, too, and ready to go home."

The ghetto store resumed its place among my memories, and I was back at the grocery laden with delicacies, amid the stifling heat of the hamsin. I opened the collar of my shirt a little wider, gave a cough, and asked with an apologetic smile, "How much do I owe you?" The grocer removed the stub of a pencil from behind his ear and started to tally on the margin of a newspaper. He was being kind and polite, in spite of what must have been a hard day for him. I paid, took my change, and, after exchanging shaloms, hoisted the plastic bag filled with foods to tickle the fussiest palate and stepped out to the street.

The sea of excited people, the flood of colored lights, and the unending stream of cars were proof that the days of the Holocaust were now part of the history books. I awakened from my horrible memories and almost agreed with the opinion voiced by many that the ghetto was a dead issue and the whole period surrounding it too far-fetched, too cruelly sadistic, to be believable today, assuming it really existed. . . . The reign of man-eating furnaces is hard for a reasonable mind to grasp, even that of someone who was a victim himself. At times, I regarded the era of crucifixions on the swastika cross as mere nightmare, devoid of any moral or human considerations. But more often it seemed to me that the present reality is but a delusive dream, and I feared that I might wake up dressed in the striped uniform, somewhere in the middle of World War II, when the command "And thou shalt love thy neighbor as thyself" was cruelly eradicated.

A huge illuminated poster advertising a movie, *Love in the Camp*, reminded me that I had promised to take my wife to the cinema that night. I started to walk faster, pushing my way through the rushing, sweating crowd. The hamsin kept adding fuel to its central

LOVE IN
THE CAMP

An Unforgettable
Story

Winner of
10 Oscars

ADULTS ONLY

heating system, and the radio announcer threatened that the heat wave would stay with us, the temperatures remaining higher than was usual for this time of year. The café customers kept fanning themselves with newspapers in an effort to cool off, and the taxi drivers waved white handkerchiefs as a sign of surrender to the hamsin.

The heat brought people out onto the balconies, and those inside relieved themselves of their clothing, as if they dwelled in the Garden of Eden.

A red light halted the traffic, creating a channel for pedestrians between the solid rows of cars. After reaching the next crossing, I walked through a dark lane, then a large square adorned with a fountain, and I found myself again on the crowded main street, where I stopped in bewilderment in front of a pharmacy. According to my recollection, there had been a watchmaker next to the pharmacy. I was sure of it! Every evening, when I passed under the clock that dictated the time of day from its lofty perch, I used to reset my watch, which wasn't the most accurate in the world. Next to it was a shoe store boasting a neon sign. Wait a minute . . .

I remembered buying some aspirin two days before. The druggist — yes, the very same as the one behind the counter now, tall and bearded, with gold-rimmed glasses — didn't have change for my large bill, and I went to the watchmaker's to ask him for change. Yes, the druggist and the watchmaker were neighbors. Their display windows were like Siamese twins. But the shop selling watches with names like Omega, Tissot, and Seiko used to be located right here, where the sidewalk leads to the dark lane. Is that possible?

No, I decided, the heat must be getting to me. . . . Probably there was a similar pharmacy farther down, and beside that one was a watchmaker and a shoe store. I had just failed to notice it before. I must get to know the area better.

Once more, I turned a searching eye toward the pharmacy in order to compare the druggist and the store fixtures with the one etched in my memory. I concluded that they must have used the same decorator for their interiors.

My curiosity aroused the suspicion of the druggist, and he came out to ask me, "Are you looking for something, sir?"

"No, nothing," I stammered, as if caught in some misdeed, and turned hastily into the adjacent lane. Without a doubt, this lane remembered the founding of the city. The houses were ancient, the pavement was worn. Compared to the teeming main street, it seemed enveloped in total darkness. One thing intrigued me — a cold wind was blowing through it, apparently coming from the sea. I looked at my watch. I still had an hour to make the cinema. I chose the lane not only to escape the druggist's suspicion or to take a shortcut, but also to satisfy my adventurous spirit as well as enjoy the cool air.

The houses were clearly old, built in an antique style. I strained my eyes in the dim light to make out any details, but found it impossible. All the same, the facades reminded me of similar houses in my native city in Europe. It must have been the coolness, the dim light, and the quiet stillness that took hold of my imagination. My thoughts went on a wild spree, as the similarity evoked fear and made me uneasy. My throat constricted, and my heart beat faster. All sorts of misgivings, based on my past experiences, came to life, together with a strong feeling of wariness born of those days. I glanced suspiciously over my shoulder. Not too far back, on the main thoroughfare, the stream of people kept moving against a ground of brightly illuminated houses and blinking neon signs.

Relieved, I marched on. I could have retraced my steps, but I was anxious to be home on time. Soon I would reach the boulevard, and from there it was only a few steps. In the meantime, the cool breeze gathered strength and broke the back of the hamsin. This was not the first time the learned weathermen had led us astray. I had to admit that I was never taken in by their forecasts, which relied on radio and television to fool us. I rebuttoned my collar and raised the shopping bag to protect my chest. Had I not known the date, I would have thought winter was on the way. In any case, I decided we should take sweaters to the cinema.

Behind the closed gates, I could see a faint flicker of yellow light in a few of the houses. I became aware of my footsteps echoing in the empty streets. People gazed at me through the darkened windows, worried expressions on their faces and fear in their eyes as they closely followed my movements. I stopped and looked back. The bright main street was already far away, and I considered turning back. My eyes tried to pierce the darkness, till I spotted a lantern among the trees. The boulevard must be close, only a few meters away, so I decided to keep going. A false surge of strength filled my throat and urged me on. Full of apprehension, I plunged ahead with long strides, until I spotted the store identified by the deceptive words DELICATESSEN AND PASTRIES. The empty window displayed a large sign in primitive print: TODAY BREAD WILL BE DISTRIBUTED, L COUPON NO. 9. And the sidewalk was covered with frozen mud under my feet. Seized with terror, I tried to turn back, but then the gate of a nearby house opened and a strange hand grabbed my sleeve and pulled me inside. My shopping bag was torn and a few items spilled on the sidewalk when the gate closed behind me.

"What are you doing on the street after the curfew? Don't you know that if you're caught, all of us will suffer? Are you exempt from following the orders of the SS commandant? Who are you anyway — are you a Jew?" All this was said in Yiddish, while shadows wrapped in shawls and torn rags threatened me with their fists and chastised me in a noisy chorus. Frightened, I covered my face with my hands in an effort to wake up, to make sure it was just a demented documentary dream. I tried to beat a retreat, but the bag with its partially spilled groceries tripped me, as in a real nightmare.

"What do you want from me? Let me out!" I screamed.

"Are you off your rocker? Where do you want to go?"

"I live not far from here, and I promised to take my wife to the cinema tonight. She's at home, waiting for me."

"A cinema?" echoed my captors in unison. After conferring in Yiddish in low tones, one of them came up to face me and asked with suspicion, "Excuse me, sir, are you not Jewish?"

"Of course I'm Jewish, but who are you?"

"If you're Jewish, where is your Star of David armband?" he

said, pointing to the one decorating his torn sleeve. Then I saw that all the others had the same bands on their arms, which they had raised during the discussion. Suddenly, the arms became petrified in midair, and everyone's parted lips remained open in silence. A rhythmic noise intruded through the closed gate, gaining in volume and getting closer. It sounded like the clatter of gears in some strange machine. I soon identified it as the dull clacking of wooden clogs, mixed with the sharp click of the hobnailed boots and the hoarse commands "Left, left, left . . ."

The sound of running feet and the muted closing of doors ended my meeting with the actors in this impromptu reconstruction of the days of the Murder of a People Syndicate, but I survived. With a single mighty leap, I reached the gate, turned the rusty latch, and opened the resisting barrier, but remained there, frozen.

By the pale light of the moon, a group of what used to be normal humans was moving along the street, a vivid reminder of those days. The SS men in their steel helmets, holding loaded machine guns, escorted the phalanx of skeletons consigned by their striped uniforms to a cruel fate. . . . For a moment, my senses, detached from reality, deceived me with inaccurate assumptions. I was watching a film borrowed from Yad Vashem, the Holocaust museum in Jerusalem, but damn it, hadn't I bought tickets to see some comedy today — yes, a comedy? . . . What's going on? Where is my wife? Where is the movie house, filled with patrons?

Suddenly, one of the zebra-striped marchers broke ranks, picked up something with a practiced movement, and resumed his place. A Nazi, true to his calling, stopped the column with a raging scream and shoved the offender out of line with the butt of his rifle. The man, whose face became deadly white, extracted from his striped folds a loaf of kimmel bread and a bar of nut-filled chocolate, while the German kicked him brutally. Following a harangue accusing international Jewry of terrorism and plotting

against the holy Reich, he fired a single shot. The victim clutched his chest and fell to the ground. All the while, the convoy of ex-human shadows stood by with indifference.

The beam of a flashlight swept the sidewalk outside the house in which I was hiding. I lay down in the dim corridor behind the front door and hugged the wall. An SS man holding a can of coffee and a package of biscuits burst in, took the stairs at a run, and attacked the door of the first apartment with the butt of his rifle. I heard screams, pleas for mercy, and the wailing of children. Glass was being smashed inside, and furniture thudded to the floor. A loud bellow, the sound of gunfire, and a desperate groan followed. Then the beam of the flashlight found the door of the apartment opposite, and the scenario was repeated. An apparition — was it a man or a hunted animal? — materialized at the top of the stairs, clutching a bag filled with red apples, a box of tea, and some potatoes. He was pursued by the SS man, who directed a burst of machine-gun fire at his back. The man barely managed to cry out, *"Shmah Yisrael"* — "Hear, O Israel" — as he rolled down the stairs, landing in a heap next to my hiding place. His hand touched my shoe, as if trying to tell me something. The killer grabbed the bag, leaped over the victim, and vanished into the night outside the gate. A resounding command, "Maaarch," activated the shuffling of the wooden clogs. "Left, left, left . . ." was heard again. Unable to react reasonably, I stood hidden behind the door, quaking with fear. Once more, I had flunked the acid test. All the tales of heroism and courage related to the free world, far away. In the face of mortal danger, I responded now exactly as I had then, with total helplessness. The atmosphere of terror turned me into a being dependent on miracles, concerned only with saving his own skin. The motto of those days was: Put your head willingly under the ax, or save yourself by any means, even at the expense of others. Despite years of polemics and oaths of defiance against the aggressors, I simply decided to flee.

I jumped over the body lying in a pool of its blood, made sure it was safe to leave my hiding place, and cast a prayerful look toward the busy main street, which lay at the end of the lane, shining like a bright star, full of promise. Encouraged by the absolute silence, I tried to move on, but my feet tripped over the snare of the Jew who had paid with his life for my kimmel loaf and the nut-filled chocolate.

On my way to the boulevard, I ignored the rules of the game, the need to administer first aid to bleeding cuts, and paid no attention to the insistent murmuring of my conscience. I was soaring at top speed, the wind whistling in my ears, my feet hardly touching the pavement. My right arm had come free from its sleeve, and my torn shirt flapped in the air. My hair obscured the bright street, which was fast approaching. I tried to brush it aside with a hand across my wet forehead, but it stuck obstinately to its perverse task. Behind me, from the lane I was fleeing, came a warning to halt, and a bullet whistled by me, then another. I didn't let up, didn't look back. They're shooting at me, the bastards; let them shoot! I'll show them the world knows all about them. Safety is very near. Every second is bringing me closer. I was covered with steaming perspiration, as the air grew warmer. The hamsin returned. The shooting continued, but now the reports were distant, and no bullets whistled over my head.

The next sound that came to my ears was the honking of car horns and the noise of people melting from the heat of the hamsin on the street full of lights and blinking neon signs. The drugstore came into view. Just one more effort, a few more steps . . .

I collapsed on the sidewalk in the middle of the crowd. All the nerves in my sweating body became powerless. Curious heads hovered over me . . . more heads. They enclosed me in a cage without air. Thrill seekers were asking: What happened to him? Where is he from? Is he drunk? High on drugs? Someone call an ambulance! Give him some water or he'll die. He must be suffering heat stroke!

Slowly, I regained my strength and rose clumsily to my feet. In a stammer, I tried to awaken a sense of morality in them: "Listen, everybody! There's a ghetto in this city. I just saw with my own eyes how SS men are killing people. The streets are flowing with the blood of innocents! Come and help! Call the police."

"Where did you see this?" they asked. "You must be crazy — that's impossible!"

"Yes, this man is obviously crazy. He has been hanging around here for some time," explained the bearded druggist. "A few minutes ago, he was eyeing my store suspiciously."

"Please, listen! I'm completely sane. Look at the lane around the corner — can't you see?" The circle surrounding me opened up. Frightened by my words, they moved aside. "Just look up the lane next to the drugstore. It's there —" My hand encountered the watchmaker's window. My other hand froze, still holding the bag full of groceries.

MONUMENTS

They have erected monuments of words
built of the finest gold bricks.
They have put the heroes of the revolts
on pedestals of basalt,
their names etched in marble by the tears of orphans
to record what the Germans did to us.

On remembrance days,
the cantors intone consolations and eulogies,
and schoolchildren act in fitting plays.
As for us, graduates of the camps,
we pledge money to save the souls.
And the new generations, who did not know the scourge,
visit the Auschwitz Chamber of Horrors to learn
what the Germans did to us.

It takes very little to remind me:
the smell of burned milk on a stove brings forth
the furnaces devouring Jews by the millions.
A bloodstained truck from the local slaughterhouse
brings forth the truckloads of victims sacrificed
by the Germans on the altars of their barbaric deities.
The skull and crossbones on poisons brings forth
the skulls that stared down at me with undisguised hatred
from the caps of the SS men.

Here, a pile of mementos
condemned to be a heap of refuse
discarded on a cleaning day,
or a loaf of black bread,
or a pair of striped pajamas, though not numbered,
a cockroach seeking shelter in a cracked wall,
the screeching of car brakes halting nearby —

these are my monuments, reminding me
of what the Germans did to us.

A parade of kindergarten children
is always accompanied by an armed monument
dressed in the green uniform of a German soldier.

And every nude woman is a living monument
to piles of nude women
fallen prey to cannibals of German descent.

THE TRIAL IN VIENNA

Background

In February 1971, my wife and I received invitations from the Austrian government to testify in the trial of the SS man Gruen, who was accused of murdering thousands of concentration camp prisoners, after subjecting them to the vilest tortures. My father, Abraham, of blessed memory, was one of his victims.

Within twenty-four hours, our mission became common knowledge among our friends and acquaintances. I had to explain to the envious ones again and again, when they came to wish us bon voyage, that it wasn't a pleasure trip. Vienna probably had a blanket of snow, and I doubted whether we could stand the winter frosts after twenty-two years of torrid hamsins. What is more, I was afraid of this master killer's effect on us when he emerged from the realm of my nightmares into real life. In addition — and this was the most important obstacle to our trip — our first grandson, whose birth filled us with joy, had a date set for his B'rith Milah, the circumcision ceremony, on the exact day of the trial.

My wife inquired at the Austrian embassy if, owing to special family circumstances, we could postpone our trip for at least ten days. The answer, given in German, was an uncompromising no. Our tickets had been issued and hotels arranged; if we didn't leave as scheduled, it would be too late and it might affect the outcome of the trial, even lead to a miscarriage of justice. Our close and not so close friends exhorted us to take advantage of this opportunity to avenge the blood of our brethren. "It's your duty to awaken the conscience of the world. Don't you remember how much you would have given in the camp to come out alive and to see the Germans defeated? Don't you know that new Hitlers are now spreading the lie that the concentration camps existed only in the sick imagination of the Jews, who invented the story in order to extort compensation from the poor German people? We must reveal to the world the truth about the neo-Nazis, who are following in their fathers' footsteps and are trying to distort the facts."

Then they added, with a wink and a whisper, that this might be our last chance to travel abroad at the expense of the Austrians. If we used our wits, we might even manage to save a few hundred schillings, which was nothing to sneeze at.

The Fateful Decision

After considering the pros and cons of a crusade against the crooked cross — including some grave prophetic warnings from friends not to leave our house — we reached a compromise solution. We would go to Vienna but would stay only long enough to give testimony; the morning after the verdict, we would return home.

Thus we would discharge our sacred duty and hurry home to enjoy our grandson. Before leaving, my wife went to the hospital to apprise the little one and his mother of our plan, the outcome of a deep inner conflict. She had expected to be only a few minutes, but it was late at night when she returned.

Preparing for the Trip

Since General Winter still had command in Vienna in February, my wife and I embarked on a project we dubbed "Prepare Your Body for the Frost." For starters, we rummaged around for cold-weather clothing among the relics of our distant past in the diaspora. After we had received our "oleh books" (documents issued to immigrants) in the old-new Holy Land, which has a semitropical climate, we no longer needed a winter wardrobe. The old clothes stayed unemployed, suffering from an inferiority complex in some hidden corner. The years erased their tracks, so, for instance, we couldn't remember the location of our brand-new galoshes, which had tasted European snow only once. Now they became a necessity. Where could we find the two pairs of mittens we had bought for our last outing on the Continent? And the earmuffs my grandmother had knitted, which we had last seen among the sewing items in the drawer? Nor did we find the long johns I had hated but would be happy to have now. If only these things could be induced to emerge from their hiding places!

Who knows where I could find my fur hat, which we used once on Purim when masquerading as Eskimos? Our parkas were likewise not to be found, having disappeared without leaving any forwarding address. In their place we took raincoats of a local make, reinforced with colorful scarves. We had carried all sorts of other polar equipment here but had similarly found no suitable employment for them. Their names didn't even appear in the latest edition of the local dictionary. And during our start in the Promised Land, they had merely been the source of ridicule. They testified to the negligence of the Zionist emissaries in failing to acquaint us with the geographical facts of the country.

We turned the moldy dust-and-cobweb-covered suitcases inside out, we delved among the stacks of antiques that had been removed from the sight of visitors; we looked in the closets and bookshelves. All we found were items we had longed for when we were younger. An album of yellowed snapshots from our past saw daylight again and showed how we looked to the ancient cameras. We uncovered the rental lease for our first apartment, whose absence had caused us to lose half of the deposit my wife felt we were entitled to when we moved. Oh, yes, and we found a rusty key that had escaped from us during the last decade, the loss of which had forced us to break and replace the lock on our safe. But my grandmother's woolen earmuffs, the galoshes, the long johns, our mittens and fur hats, managed to evade us.

"Nu, let's be sensible; do we need such a rich wardrobe for only three days?" I said to my wife. "It's not as if we're heading for the wilderness. Anything we need, we can buy."

But I met with stiff opposition. According to her prophetic soul, you never knew what might happen. This was not a jaunt to Petach Tikvah but a trip to another country. So she stuffed the suitcases, continually reopening the lid and adding another item that struck me as superfluous. At last, I managed to close the swollen bags, affixed tags with our name in the plastic windows, and announced triumphantly that the preparations for the trip were complete.

Travel Tension

El Al flight 457 was departing at seven zero zero hours, according to the recorded announcement. This meant that we ought to be at the airport by at least 6 A.M. Thus we had to get up by at least 4 A.M. to leave the house by 5 A.M., which meant that we had three hours to grab some sleep, as I made this calculation at 1 A.M. For the sake of three hours' sleep, it wasn't worthwhile changing into pajamas. We could just nap on the sofa until it was time to leave. However, my wife's opinion was different. I argued that it was a waste of time to dress and undress, and something was more likely to get forgotten, God forbid. She, on the other hand, said that only cave dwellers sleep in their clothes, a practice that breeds all sorts of bugs. She undressed, donned her pajamas, and went to sleep as usual in our bed, as if this were an ordinary quiet night, as if time weren't limited, as if the plane would wait for us, if need be.

In contrast to my wife's elegant notions, I tried to do what was urgently required. There wouldn't be enough time when we woke even to brush our teeth, so it was best to be ready ahead of time. To prove my point, I filled my pockets with the essential papers: passports, tickets, hotel confirmation, a wallet stuffed with dollars and schillings, and a list of addresses in Israel to which we would send attractive and tempting postcards — let them be green with envy! I dialed for a wake-up call, which turned out to be superfluous, as I didn't close an eye for a second.

To the Airport

We took a taxi to the airport, and my wife murmured a blessing: "May it be in a propitious hour." Squeezed between the suitcases and a few smaller bags, I looked for my left arm in order to check the "propitious hour" on my watch. In a voice full of tension and concern, I announced, "A quarter to six. Do you think we can jump into the plane while it's taxiing for takeoff?"

In answer, my wife addressed the driver. "Mister, we're in a hurry. Can you step on it?" Without checking to see whether her request was heeded, she started to make a list of the things we had forgotten to take: "Pictures of the children, the box of medicines, the address book, and something very important, which I can't recall just now."

"Would you like to return home for just a few seconds?" I whispered. I was beginning to feel uncomfortable in two pairs of underwear, the long-sleeved woolen shirt with a colorful tie, and the coat with its liner. In spite of the early hour, the hamsin was heating up already, and I consoled myself that we would be far away by the time it reached its peak. In the meantime, the beads of perspiration on my forehead were proof enough that our improvised winter wardrobe was not suitable for this country. Would it be suitable for the Vienna winter?

"Remove your hat," ordered my wife. "Loosen your tie and try to remove your coat. You're sweating something awful."

"First I'd have to get out from under the pile of bags. Besides, I want to save some of this heat for the days ahead," I answered disobediently.

Looking into the Past

"We are now flying over Greece," said the stewardess, while handing out candies. "Breakfast will be served soon. How do you like your eggs — soft- or hard-boiled, or in an omelet?" Both of us opted for omelets. I was very hungry, as the frenzied rush and preflight tension had left no time for eating.

My wife was concerned with a more important matter — my court appearance. "Don't forget how necessary it is to say that you saw with your own eyes how Gruen shot your father to death. You were standing close by and remember it clearly."

"But that isn't accurate; I just saw Gruen leading my father away, and I heard a gun being fired. Then I saw, from a distance, my father lying dead in the sand." I spoke slowly, reading with difficulty the faded pages fluttering in my memory.

"It doesn't matter how it happened; nobody can deny it. Just say that you saw — otherwise, your testimony will be worthless." She made a small circle with her finger on her forehead, to indicate that she was dealing with a dolt. "The judge is liable to conclude that someone else killed your father, or that he wasn't killed at all — do you understand?"

"But I can't change facts," I persisted, while opening the table for the tray of food that the stewardess was holding over my head. My wife started on her meal at once, but I retreated into my past, which lay buried under almost thirty years of other events.

This is how it happened: One spring day, I drew a few signs for the Jewish police and was rewarded with an egg. I had forgotten what to do with it, how I was to eat it. Seeing my hesitation, one of the cops helped me. He broke the shell and poured its contents directly on the tin top of a stove that stood in the middle of the room. Then he lifted the dirty charred egg with a spoon and handed it to me on a piece of newspaper. "Eat, eat, it's very good," he said. "Bon appétit."

In spite of my gnawing hunger, I didn't touch the tempting delicacy. I ran to my father's hut in order to give him a treat, but he was not to be found. I asked the barracks elder, "Where is my father?" He answered with a single word: "Gone."

"Excuse me, where did he go? When will he be back?" My naive questions angered the honorable gentleman, and he yelled at me, "Don't you know what 'gone' means? He's gone and is no more." Then he added in a softer voice: "Gruen took him away just a minute ago, you know where."

The egg slipped off the paper, and I felt it hit my shoe. I started to run after my father, who was on his final journey on earth. I saw from afar how Gruen pushed him down a slope, holding the rifle at his back. I kept running and cried in despair, "Kill me too, kill me too!" As my father walked toward his death, his stooped back obscured the view. I didn't feel the broken road under my feet, or the sharp stones, nor did I see the people looking on with compassion. I wasn't even aware that I was waving the egg-stained newspaper over my head. My cries became an inhuman hoarse bellow. I was getting closer, but suddenly someone pulled me aside, held my head, and embraced my neck with his arms while hugging me close. I heard the familiar snap, like a hand clap, and it was over. When the man released my head from his embrace, I stood paralyzed, unable to lift my feet. I saw Gruen kick my father's corpse until it fell into a hole in the ground and the excavator covered it with earth. The man who forced me to go on living was my friend Isaac Stern. He consoled me by saying that fate willed it so and added, "Suppose he killed you too. Nu, you would be one more victim. But if you live, and the times change, you'll be able to avenge your father's death, maybe."

The stewardess collected the tray with the cold omelet, the coffee, and the rolls, all untouched, and asked, "Are you ill? Shall I call the doctor?"

"No, thanks; it'll pass. I just remembered a sad event and lost my appetite." I looked out the round window at the expanse of sky, in which the bright sun was embedded. I turned toward my wife. "Look — this is the same sky as ours and the same sun; you can see the reflection of the hamsin in its face. It started escorting us at the airport. If it keeps chasing after us, the Vienna winter can't possibly survive for long."

The Parting from the Sun

Our sun, which had accompanied us all the way, stayed above the puffy clouds while we slid through a dense fog, straight into the dreary, sad winter. The loudspeaker prepared us for the cold reception awaiting us in Vienna. The ground temperature was minus fifteen degrees and the weather exceptionally stormy for this time of year. Indeed, winter was waiting outside the round window. It seemed as though it had been waiting for us for twenty years. A nervous wind shook the naked black trees standing amid the swirling snow on the frozen ground. They looked like unwanted old acquaintances who had come to greet us — the guests from the land of spring — with a look of dark contempt on their faces.

As we got off the plane, I was assaulted by a frigid gust of hostile wind. It sprayed my face with icy pellets, pinched my ears, and invited itself inside my trembling coat. The remnants of the hamsin, which had promised to keep my heart warm, retreated into the plane, which soon would take off for home.

We went by streetcar to the hotel, through gray streets lined with gray houses under gray skies, our mood gray. Vienna reminded me of Krakow, where my youth lies buried among the victims of the war. Massive buildings with old-style facades, people in a perpetual hurry dressed in furs and exhaling clouds of steam. A layer of snow made a brave attempt to conceal from tourist eyes the ugliness that reminded me of winters lingering in my memory.

The sound of German words, and the Gothic lettering on the signs and posters, steered my mind in a familiar direction. At one of the streetcar stops, a policeman got on. He looked like an exact replica of a Hitler-era cop — the same cap, uniform, and belt buckle, and even the same facial expression. At the sight of him, I jumped up and was going for the exit, when my wife brought me back to reality.

"Have you gone mad, or are you just pretending to be an idiot?" she berated me in Polish. This attracted the attention of a few presumed Nazis.

"I'm scared. I have a feeling we're back in the ghetto and the camp," I whispered. "Will we ever feel the Israeli hamsin again?"

The Return to the Past

That afternoon, we left the hotel to inhale the winter air of the metropolis. It was hard for my lungs to breathe in the frost. Their memory short, they had forgotten even the severest cold. I felt clumsy in clothing that had never become familiar with winter. I chafed my ears and my nose, which was blowing steam. I tried to draw my hat lower over my freezing head and to fool my neck with a felt scarf, but to no avail.

I was inside the freezer compartment of a refrigerator. The only thing that reassured me was the thought that there was a hamsin back home and the perspiring citizens of Tel Aviv were sitting in sidewalk cafés, enjoying all sorts of ice cream, sweet, colorful, and aromatic. My soul was atoning for all the curses I had heaped on the scorching sun, the impossibly crowded buses, and the torrid hamsin, whose like even the oldest inhabitants couldn't remember.

We were walking on the main drag, Maria Hilfe Strasse, which was enveloped in a dense fog. Behind the windowpanes, decorated by Jack Frost with shimmery white designs, life went on. Every time a door opened, it was like lifting the lid of a boiling kettle to let out the steam, which disappeared immediately in the cold.

Having no alternative, we entered a supermarket, a pair of snowmen who needed to be defrosted. We lingered over postcards depicting the city at a time when it was free of snow and enjoying the summer sun.

A blond salesgirl, a model of politeness and practiced courtesy, offered to help us. Her Gothic dialect and blue eyes awoke in me the dormant image of the SS woman who was in charge of the women's barracks. I stepped back in order to appease my conscience, which claimed attention. But there I saw, in the guise of the sales manager, a tall SS officer whose hobby was murder. The same

double chin, the same neatly trimmed and shaven neck, the same haircut and low forehead. Frightened out of my wits, I rushed to the door, which was opened by a huge ruffian, his rimless glasses clearly meant to disguise the cold cruelty of his face. Winter was waiting outside, with its pure snow blowing the same icy pellets in my face, the same winter of yore, erstwhile ally of the Nazis.

When my wife emerged from the store with a package in her hand, I was a real snowman, complete with a reddish carrot nose and gray pebbles for eyes.

The First Night

The central heating in our room was on strike. The concierge promised to send a repairman; we could change rooms only the next day, as the hotel was completely full. "I just remembered an important item I forgot to bring," said my wife, as she emerged from the kitchenette. "The electric heater for water. We could have warmed up a little with some tea. You said we didn't have to bring anything."

"And I think if you had brought the kettle, the heater, and a can of kerosene, we could not only have enjoyed a cup of tea, we could have heated the room as well. If they don't repair the radiator, I'm going to bed in my coat, hat, and shoes."

"Don't even joke about pulling something like that. They're liable to think we came straight from the jungle," said my wife, while shivering on the armchair between two blankets. "They'll be here soon to fix the radiator."

It was after midnight when the technician showed up, and the room became warm a half hour later. However, when we undressed and went to bed, the anti-Semitic radiator refused to let us sleep. It squealed, knocked, and whistled, and when it got tired of annoying us, the heat vanished too. General Winter took command in our room again while we lay snug in bed, and he threatened to freeze anyone daring to put a foot on the floor without his permission.

The Way to the Courthouse

The hotel manager suggested that we take a taxi to the courthouse. "On a day like this, your life is in danger on the street," he said, as he dialed the taxi station.

When we heard the sound of a horn, we held our breaths and jumped straight into the cab, which was complaining in the snow storm. My wife gave directions to the driver in the language that had once served the masters: "To the High Court of Justice!" The cab started to shimmy over the street covered with frozen gray slush. Not only the cab was shaking; we too shivered, from cold and fear.

Suddenly, I felt hot, terribly hot, as if boiling lava had escaped from the volcano of excitement and invaded my chilled body. "Look in the rearview mirror," I whispered to my wife in an effort to pass on some of the heat. "Who does he look like, with his little mustache and the strand of hair on his forehead?" She opened her eyes and mouth and cried out carelessly, "Hitler!" The driver turned his Hitlerian head around and thanked her for the compliment.

The Trial

The cold, serious eyes of His Honor the judge observed me from beneath the wings of a giant black iron bird, which loomed over the central wall of the courtroom dedicated to the scales of justice. Being used to a state symbol in the form of a menorah on a blue background, I stood hypnotized before the Austrian eagle, an obvious relative of the Nazi's vampirelike emblem. They looked alike: Both belonged to the family of birds of prey, having bent beaks, sharp claws, and a single eye searching for a victim.

The jurors, seated on the right, gazed at me while trying to convey a feeling of righteousness. On the left sat my father's murderer, who had killed, without a shred of pity, thousands of people whose only sin was being Jewish. It took courage for me to look

at his face, and I managed it only when the judge asked me, "Does the witness recognize the accused?"

I turned toward him with hesitation and the fear of a concentration camp graduate. And now my vengeful eyes peered into the pleading eyes of the wreck that had once been a savage and bloodthirsty beast.

"Yes, this is the man who murdered thousands of Jews in the Plaszow concentration camp, including my father, Abraham, of blessed memory," I declared, in a voice that gradually gained in strength. The interpreter kept translating my experiences, which I related in Hebrew, though I was forced to resort to expressions in German when there were no equivalents. These were expressions like *SS, Transport, Aktion, Selektion, Appellplatz, Kapo, Lager* (camp), and *Fassung,* idioms of German creation that have now become a part of international usage but can be effective only in their original context.

I described the blood-soaked career of the SS man Gruen, the terror and fear he inspired when he appeared on the *Appellplatz* or rode his white steed in the New District, and the various atrocities he supervised. I spoke about the way he killed my father, about the fried egg, my desire to die together with him, and the way my friend Isaac Stern saved me. My testimony didn't appear to affect the jurors. One of them asked, "In order to prove the truth of what he is saying, can the witness name the date of his father's death? What were the month, day, and hour of the event?"

"Dear sir," I addressed him, "don't you know that the Germans changed the names of the Jewish prisoners to numbers, which they tattooed on their arms? They shaved their heads, dressed them in striped uniforms, and turned them into anonymous creatures, devoid of rights and character. This arrangement was in force while we were enclosed in the death camp by means of electrified barbed-wire fences. Timepieces and calendars had been removed, so that the days of the week became one long period of hard labor whose divisions were marked by the sound of bugles. There were no designated days, no measures of time. Our time couldn't be measured by ordinary means, which were denied to us. I can only say that my father was murdered by Gruen on a spring morning, a short time after our arrival at the concentration camp. I can't even define for myself the date on which to light the annual candle in his memory."

Then another expert stood up and asked, "How many meters separated the witness from the place where Gruen allegedly shot his father?"

"I am not able to estimate the distance today. I was small at the time, and the distances looked greater to me."

"How old were you then?"

"I was twenty-three years old."

"Is a person of twenty-three considered small?" asked the juror with scorn, in the hope of catching me in a lie.

"Sir, if you lived four years under the Nazis, you would also not grow, for lack of nourishment. I grew only as a result of medical treatment, at the age of twenty-five, when I was put on a normal diet."

There were no further questions, so my mission was accomplished. But this was only the beginning of a mysterious set of circumstances. When my wife entered the hall, I was sitting in the gallery, an audience of one. During her testimony, she addressed Gruen directly in German: "You participated in the 'actions' together with the other SS men. You killed thousands of people without reason. You are the man that —"

Gruen rose from his seat, raised his walking stick like a gun, pointed it at the judge, and cried out in an insulted tone, "This is a lie, this is a lie. I never shot any Jews. I always aimed in the opposite direction or just fired at random like this. . . ."

Then he turned and pointed the cane at the gallery, straight at me. I felt a stab in my heart, as if he were carrying out the wish I had made twenty-eight years earlier.

Going Home?

The overwhelming fear that had lain dormant in the subconscious recesses of my brain since the war suddenly burst free. This fear had gripped me since I set foot on Austrian soil. In my naïveté, I was hoping that after the decisive test, it would return voluntarily to its hiding place in my memory, to the nightmare section of my youth, occupied by the Nazi conquest. But no matter how I tried, I couldn't evade it. On the contrary, it now started to dog me. My body trembled, my teeth chattered, and I was bereft of my spiritual equilibrium. Restlessness and insecurity took hold of my thoughts. The European delicacies failed to arouse my appetite; sightseeing in Vienna failed to tempt me. The famous museums and even the color TV, new in those days, that stood proudly in the hotel lobby couldn't entertain me. A faintness buzzed in my ears, and my veins fed the beats into my heart, one by one.

In the evening, I felt my vision getting blurred. Each eye became independent, and I saw double. I wiped my glasses, but it wasn't their fault. My voice sounded distant to me, as if uttered by a strange mouth. Were my ears out of tune or sealed up? The hotel manager transferred us to a heated room, but I couldn't get rid of an odd feeling.

"You see," I said to my wife, "I'm Gruen's last victim — he's carrying out my wish of years ago."

"What are you babbling about? Do you believe in all these silly superstitions?" She tried to comfort me, but she eyed me with growing concern.

In the morning, I was almost too weak to get up. I dressed with great difficulty, and my feet refused to obey me. Supported by my wife, I took the elevator to the lobby, where our luggage was ready for "transport" to the airport. While my wife went to call a cab, the "action" began. Outside, people trudged in the snow among scattered suitcases, corpses, and the cries of children. Gruen stood in the midst of it, firing his gun. Then he turned toward the hotel entrance and aimed straight at me. The wind whistled with the sound of a shofar on Rosh Hashanah, the Jewish New Year.

Someone led me over the quaking floor, to a room with trembling walls, and went to call a doctor. Someone else was massaging my forehead when "Herr Doktor" came into the swirling room, measured my blood pressure, and said in German, "Please wait a moment." Then he left in a hurry.

The Kidnapping

My wife was standing by the window when two tall men in SS uniforms, wearing the green hats with cords on the visors, grabbed me under the arms and led me toward the exit. My frightened wife started to shout in German, "Where are you taking my husband? Where are you taking my husband?" She tried to block the door, but a blond woman in a black leather coat, an SS coat, held her back and said in the tone of an order, "He is coming with us, but you stay here."

The two SS men hustled me along the corridor so fast that my feet hardly touched the floor. Instead of the cab that was to take us to the airport, there was a green van with a Gothic inscription under the Red Cross symbol — or was it a swastika? The figure of my wife was fading in the fog that seemed to envelop the whole world. I tried to defend myself, to cry out, but my strength failed me. My wife was shouting at the van as it started to pull away, and it halted. Then she got in and sat by my side. Her face and coat were spattered with the dirty slush.

They're taking me to the concentration camp, I thought. I made sure that I could recite in German my prison number, 69084.

The Hospital

On his first visit, the doctor exploded my delusions and brought me back to reality. He was sure, without the shadow of a doubt, that the excitement of the last few days had caused my erratic pulse and a blood pressure of 210 over 130, which is very high. This condition was the source of my odd feeling, my optical disorder, and the hearing disturbances, and had made it necessary to rush me to the hospital.

"Doctor," I asked cautiously, "the two SS men and the SS woman who kidnapped me from the hotel, were they also a figment of my sick imagination? And the cops and soldiers on the street, do they just *look* like Nazis?" With utmost courtesy, the doctor explained that after the war, thousands of uniforms were left in the military stores, and it was thought a pity to destroy them. Therefore, after slight alterations, they were put to good use.

"For understandable reasons, you are sensitive to some appearances," he added. "I suggest that you see a psychiatrist on your return home. In the meantime, try not to get excited or worry about things. Here we are treating you only for high blood pressure, which will take some time."

The "some time" lasted a whole month. There were five other patients in my hospital room. My wife was kept in the women's section for two weeks because of mental stress induced by my illness and the imaginary SS men and SS woman.

A Visitor to the Sick

After a troubled effort at groping for some straw to hang on to, I concluded that I had fallen into a trap and nothing could help me. I subjected myself to a strict self-administered test and graded the results with a "D," accompanied by three exclamation points. My only chance was to resign myself to my less than promising fate. For two days, I had been lying in a foreign place, among strange people who spoke a language I did not understand.

Following those two days of gnawing doubt, a man in an elegant suit, wearing a black tie adorned with a diamond stud, came to my bed and asked in not very elegant Hebrew, "What is it that you want from me?"

"Excuse me, sir," I answered, with unconcealed joy. "If you

identify yourself, I'll tell you what you can do for me." The mysterious visitor opened his mouth in anger: "Who am *I*? Who are *you* to bother me during my working hours? Do you think I have nothing more important to do than to visit you?"

In my confusion, I imagined that my high blood pressure was causing me to see a phantom again. I got a grip on myself, so as not to go flying off my delicately balanced rocker, and asked with astonishment, "Sir, are you from the Israeli embassy in Vienna? The doctor in charge said he would inform them that two of their citizens are undergoing treatment at this hospital. That's all! Since you're already here, may I ask that you inform my family that we finished our testimony at the trial and — "

The deputy ambassador didn't let me finish my request, maybe my last one ever, and scolded me in fury. "We are busy with many more important matters and have no time for pests who are roaming around the world. Don't bother us with your silly problems." Then he left, without wishing us a speedy recovery or bidding us an indifferent *shalom*.

That was that. We were alone at the end of the world, bereft of help, money, or hope. Meanwhile, our new grandson was waiting for his B'rith Milah, and nobody knew where to contact us.

A more considerate visitor was Oskar Schindler, who suddenly appeared with a large bag of food and a big smile. Mr. Schindler, who lived in Vienna, took the time to visit us at least twice. It was he who informed our family in Israel of our whereabouts.

The Treatment

Every morning, a nurse measured my blood pressure and temperature, asked about my bowel movement, and drew lines up and down the chart hanging over my head. Once a week, I was given an EKG,

Oskar Schindler

blood test, and an X-ray examination. Every afternoon, a nurse called out the names of the patients in a loud voice, and after getting a "Jawohl" in reply, she searched for Herr Doktor's instructions in a dog-eared notebook. Then she removed a vial or a pillbox from an ancient tray she was carrying and spilled a few pills into her palm, transferring them to a fold of paper. One patient, who was already mobile, gave the rest their medicines, without explaining how to take them, without even caring if they did.

The food was the same for all, without distinction as to age or illness. It was ladled from a steel pot in equal measures, and there was no way to get anything different. Once, after tasting what had been dished up, I complained that it had too much salt, which was forbidden to me. The orderly took the plate away, gave me a distasteful glance, and, without uttering a word, placed it on another patient's table. I got nothing in its place.

When I was finally allowed to leave my bed, I had to stand naked in line, in order to wash in the only sink in the room, without worrying whether any women were about. We made our own beds; the linens were changed once a week. When we had to use the toilet, which worked only when the pipes weren't frozen, we had to wrap ourselves in a blanket to keep warm. Most of the doctors who came from time to time paid no attention to me. One of them spoke Polish and would come to see me furtively, either late at night or early in the morning.

Getting Acquainted

After ten days in the hospital, my wife visited me for the first time. To me this was like seeing a light at the end of a tunnel. Until then, I had been in despair, like a stone that couldn't be turned. Afterward, I started to feel human again.

We started to discuss ways of extricating ourselves from this situation. My wife spoke with my roommates, with whom I could communicate only nonverbally, being unable to use their language. In spite of the brave efforts of my German teacher in high school, that language had always refused to lodge itself in my brain. My good intentions, the pleas of my parents, and the threat of a failing mark on my diploma were to no avail. Even when my life depended on it, I couldn't absorb the language of my masters. Obviously, the German tongue despised me as well, and its speech became an exercise in mutual hatred, to which there was no solution.

In conversations with my wife, each one of my neighbors opened his own Pandora's box. None of them tried to conceal his sadistic past during the Hitler era. All had been SS men in the concentration camps or other prison compounds. They spoke nostalgically about those "glorious good old days." They praised the great Führer and expressed the belief that all was not lost, their truth would be restored to rule the world, and then . . . Ho-ho-ho.

Finally, they asked who we were, and my wife opened their eyes. "We are from Israel, and we came to testify against a notorious Nazi. . . ." This severed our contact with them for good. They tried to obscure their experiences and explain their conduct as just carrying out orders. But nothing could disguise their polluted minds; no perfume could hide the smell of rot in their souls.

I understood that I had fallen into a pit of snakes and scorpions. My fears emerged again. Would we ever return to our home in Israel?

Going Home

I was discharged with a warning that I had not fully recovered and would require further hospital treatment in Israel. I spent two more days in bed at the hotel, then away to the airport!

We had no regrets about leaving Vienna. On the bus, I kept my eyes closed to avoid gazing at the snow-covered streets and at the cops and soldiers in the SS uniforms left over from the war. In my heart, I saw fur-swathed Viennese waiting patiently for the coming summer and the return of the Nazi regime beneath skies that had been beclouded for us before the Final Solution, were so at present, and would be in the future.

The El Al plane was packed. To me, the crew came to symbolize sincere courtesy, and the other passengers seemed even closer than the members of my family. After a month in the diaspora, I grabbed hungrily at the Hebrew newspaper, printed in the Hebrew alphabet and devoted to Hebrew topics. It was funny — the weather forecast never used to interest me, but now I swallowed every word. "Look, there's a hamsin wind today and higher than usual temperatures. Isn't that nice? At last, we can warm up," I said to my wife.

The plane taxied down a runway covered with frozen gray slush and snow. It made a last turn over the gloomy terminal, over the ancient houses with their antique facades, above the church spires and the sharp outlines of roofs hidden under blankets of snow. We pierced the ceiling of this sad world and passed through a layer of dirty woolen tiers of insulation, and then — hup! — we were already in a world of warm light, amid the smiling sun hung in space under bright blue skies. I wanted to open the window, to breathe in the torrid air, to feel at home. My wife tried to calm me with a gentle cough, pointed to her left breast, and whispered in my ear, "Your heart, careful with your heart. Don't forget what the doctor said."

We took a cab home. It was a pleasant early-spring night. But the made-in-Israel air proved too dense for me. My lungs had to get used to it again. Even after rolling down the window and unbuttoning my collar, I couldn't catch my breath. I opened my mouth, but

the air wouldn't enter. My wife told the driver about our adventures in Europe, all in the past tense: we saw, heard, felt, feared. And I felt as if I was walking on my own Via Dolorosa, all in the present tense: I see, hear, feel, fear; there's an annoying buzzing in my ears; I have disturbances of vision, irregular heartbeats. All the symptoms I had smuggled in from abroad without a customs declaration began to bother me again.

Two days later, in the middle of a hamsin night, I was taken to the Beilinson Hospital in a screaming ambulance. The doctor on duty in the emergency ward again recorded a blood pressure of 210 over 130 and an irregular pulse.

Closing the Circle

I didn't sleep that night. Everything in me was crying out. I started wondering if I should have not gone to the trial. I had involved myself, without compulsion, in a series of inhuman experiences that were still unresolved and had deducted a month from my life. Who knew if it was worth the pain?

Had I not gone to Vienna, I would have been spared the annoyances and discomforts, but then I would have been haunted forever by the fact that I was a son who had refused to avenge the death of his father. My father would appear in my dreams to scold and berate me. Now that I had done my duty, would my testimony influence the decision of the court? Did I comport myself properly? Would this signify the closing of a circle?

Every time I forced my eyelids shut, they opened immediately by themselves, to let my eyes focus on the small area of the ceiling lit by the dim night lamp.

In the morning, the smiling nurses came to wish a good morning to those whom fate had placed here. They brought fresh linens and pajamas. Then they started their daily struggle against the will of nature. One of them, Rachel, served me a cup of tea, but then she read the chart over my head and apologized for not knowing that I had to fast. After pouring the tea down the sink, she returned to remove the gooseneck bottle from under my bed and asked, "Why haven't you provided a sample for urinalysis?"

"I'm new here, so I didn't know, and nobody told me. Everything is so clean and sterile, I simply didn't dare on my own. I'm feeling confused, because I came from a hospital that was sad and depressing. Your warmth and the friendliness, encouragement, and helpfulness here are astonishing. I'm afraid I haven't quite regained my emotional balance after my experiences abroad."

She gave an all-embracing smile, patted my hand, and said quietly, in a silky voice, "It's all right. You did well by going there, and it's nice to see you back. You will be completely well yet." With these words, she departed. At that moment, I knew that my balance sheet would be enriched by what I did for my father's memory. My suffering was just an atonement and a self-sacrifice on the altar of justice. I felt that my health, lost in a nervous breakdown, was coming back to fill my being.

When the doctor came on his rounds, I showed him the bottles of yellow and red pills I had been given. "We can't continue with the Viennese treatment. We follow the American system, while theirs is European," he explained.

"What's the difference?" I asked, and immediately regretted the question, thinking that I was about to be subjected to a medical lecture. "In Europe, they use composite drugs. As you can see, it says here that this pill contains three ingredients, including Librium, which can harm you. In this country, each drug is pure. Thus we can check whether the medicine is doing you good or harm. I hope our drugs will lower your blood pressure within three to four days."

That really happened — I went home after four days. The day before I left, when my nurse brought the lunch ordered by the doctor, I said to her, "Thank you, Nurse Rachel. You helped me when you spoke the words I'll never forget: 'You did well by going there, and it's nice to see you back. You will be completely well yet.' They were like words my father would have spoken. I've written in my notebook all I know about you: that your name is Rachel and you live in Ramle. Would you please fill in your family name and your address? I'd like to write to you when I get home."

Nurse Rachel took the pen and wrote "Abraham" as the family name and "67 Ben-Ezrah Street" underneath. When she finished, I saw the smile on her lips quickly turn into a look of concern. "What happened? You've become pale. Aren't you feeling well? I'll call the intern."

"No, no, that's not necessary," I protested. "I just got excited when you wrote your name. Abraham was my father's name."

Rachel Abraham

Ramle

Ezra 67

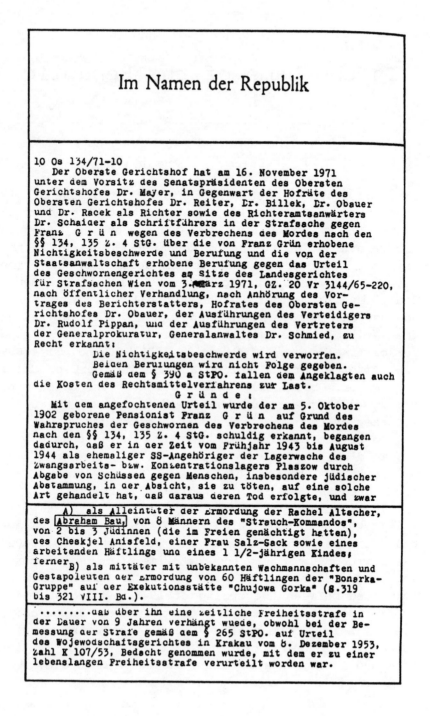

Im Namen der Republik

10 Os 134/71-10

Der Oberste Gerichtshof hat am 16. November 1971 unter dem Vorsitz des Senatspräsidenten des Obersten Gerichtshofes Dr. Mayer, in Gegenwart der Hofräte des Obersten Gerichtshofes Dr. Reiter, Dr. Billek, Dr. Obauer und Dr. Racek als Richter sowie des Richteramtsanwärters Dr. Schaider als Schriftführers in der Strafsache gegen Franz G r ü n wegen des Verbrechens des Mordes nach den §§ 134, 135 Z. 4 StG. über die von Franz Grün erhobene Nichtigkeitsbeschwerde und Berufung und die von der Staatsanwaltschaft erhobene Berufung gegen das Urteil des Geschwornengerichtes am Sitze des Landesgerichtes für Strafsachen Wien vom 3. März 1971, GZ. 20 Vr 3144/65-220, nach öffentlicher Verhandlung, nach Anhörung des Vortrages des Berichterstatters, Hofrates des Obersten Gerichtshofes Dr. Obauer, der Ausführungen des Verteidigers Dr. Rudolf Pippan, und der Ausführungen des Vertreters der Generalprokuratur, Generalanwaltes Dr. Schmied, zu Recht erkannt:

Die Nichtigkeitsbeschwerde wird verworfen.
Beiden Berufungen wird nicht Folge gegeben.
Gemäß dem § 390 a StPO. fallen dem Angeklagten auch die Kosten des Rechtsmittelverfahrens zur Last.

G r ü n d e :

Mit dem angefochtenen Urteil wurde der am 5. Oktober 1902 geborene Pensionist Franz G r ü n auf Grund des Wahrspruches der Geschwornen des Verbrechens des Mordes nach den §§ 134, 135 Z. 4 StG. schuldig erkannt, begangen dadurch, daß er in der Zeit vom Frühjahr 1943 bis August 1944 als ehemaliger SS-Angehöriger der Lagerwache des Zwangsarbeits- bzw. Konzentrationslagers Plaszow durch Abgabe von Schüssen gegen Menschen, insbesondere jüdischer Abstammung, in der Absicht, sie zu töten, auf eine solche Art gehandelt hat, daß daraus deren Tod erfolgte, und zwar

A) als Alleintäter der Ermordung der Rachel Altscher, des Abraham Bau, von 8 Männern des "Strauch-Kommandos", von 2 bis 3 Jüdinnen (die im Freien genächtigt hatten), des Cheskjel Anisfeld, einer Frau Salz-Sack sowie eines arbeitenden Häftlings und eines 1 1/2-jährigen Kindes; ferner

B) als Mittäter mit unbekannten Wachmannschaften und Gestapoleuten der Ermordung von 60 Häftlingen der "Bonerka-Gruppe" auf der Exekutionsstätte "Chujowa Gorka" (S.319 bis 321 VIII. Bd.).

.........daß über ihn eine zeitliche Freiheitsstrafe in der Dauer von 9 Jahren verhängt wurde, obwohl bei der Bemessung der Strafe gemäß dem § 265 StPO. auf Urteil des Wojewodschaftsgerichtes in Krakau vom 6. Dezember 1953, Zahl K 107/53, Bedacht genommen wurde, mit dem er zu einer lebenslangen Freiheitsstrafe verurteilt worden war.

In the Name of the Republic

10 0s 134/71-10

The High Court of Justice, presided over by the president of the High Court Dr. Mayer and a panel consisting of Dr. Reiter, Dr. Billek, Dr. Obauer, and Dr. Racek as the recording judge, sat on November 16, 1971, in the criminal case against Franz Gruen, accused of the crime of murder according to sections 134, 135 of the Penal Code, in the matter of the appeal of Franz Gruen against the indictment and sentence and the reversal of the verdict of the jury at the District Court of Vienna for criminal cases, of March 3, 1971, file no. 3144/65-220. After a public hearing and the delivery of Chief Justice Dr. Obauer, the presentation of the defense by Dr. Rudolf Pippan, and the presentation of the State Attorney Dr. Schmied, the court has decided:

To reject the plea for quashing the sentence,

To disallow the two appeals,

To impose the cost of the trial on the accused, according to section 390 of the Criminal Law.

The reasons:

In the sentence, which was the subject of the appeal, the pensioner Franz Gruen, born October 5, 1902, was convicted by a jury for the crime of murder, according to sections 134, 135 of the Penal Code, which he committed between the spring of 1943 and August 1944, as a former SS man and guard in the forced labor camp, i.e., Plaszow Concentration Camp, by shooting people, especially of Jewish origin, for the purpose of killing them and acting in a way that caused them to die.

A) He was personally guilty of murdering Rachel Altscher, Abraham Bau, eight men of the "Strauch Kommandos," 2-3 Jewesses (who slept under the open sky), Cheskjel Anisfeld, one Frau Salz-Sack, one of the prisoners among the workers, one child aged 1 1/2 years, and more.

B) As an accessory to the murder by unknown guards and Gestapo agents of 60 prisoners from the "Bonarka Group" at the execution place of "Gorka Chujowa" (pp. 319 to 321 VIII. bd).

. . . that he received a sentence of 9 years in prison, although, in passing the sentence according to section 265 of the Penal Code, it was taken in consideration that on December 8, 1953, file no. 107/53 in the District Court of Krakow, he was sentenced to life imprisonment.

THE LONGING

It happened on an evening that was yet to come,
when the compressed air in my chest
turned seconds into spans of eternity.

I measured your figure with my own,
counted your eyelashes with the tip of my tongue,
and, hungering for you, recited your virtues from memory.

The world spoke from a distance with the muted voice of a radio,
played through a wall on a soundless piano,
and spread a wide curtain behind me.

I am a pendulum aflame,
I've built lofty towers of flowery words, quietly, quietly.
My trembling lips wandered over yours,
your curls embraced my throat,
uttering a prayer of longing.

Now my hand is already next to yours,
and a practiced smile fidgets
between the eyebrows.
And the radio is ordering up tomorrow's weather,
and behind the wall the pianist is in a frenzy,
when the fading moon dares to lift the curtain.

A nosy busybody looking in
whispers, What will happen this night,
    which has already vanished?